JESUS, PERSONS,

AND THE

KINGDOM OF GOD

JESUS, PERSONS,
AND THE
KINGDOM OF GOD

by
Royce Gordon Gruenler

BETHANY PRESS · UNITED CHURCH PRESS

To Grace, my wife,
so aptly named

Preface

THE KINGDOM OF GOD is one of the metaphors in the teaching of Jesus that invite us to explore the inexhaustible world of Deity and personal meaning. It is also the most encompassing of all the pictorial figures of Jesus. We are no sooner attracted to it than we find it leading us now here, now there, into one discovery upon another. It is the symbol of a limitless realm; and more, an invitation to come to know something of the One whose kingship it symbolizes.

This book was not written for me and the Muses, as the saying goes. I had a more urgent and practical purpose in mind: to present Jesus' metaphor of the kingdom as a sign and intimation of the profound meanings of personal existence. I found that there was nothing quite to order for my undergraduate students (or, for that matter, for any inquiring person) that encompassed recent trends in biblical thought as well as the scintillating thought of contemporary philosophers such as Marcel, Wittgenstein, Polanyi, Merleau-Ponty, Whitehead, Hartshorne, Ricoeur. For I have come to cherish them as co-explorers in this inexhaustible and mysterious kingdom of reality, feeling that they have much to say about the kingdom of God and how we theologians might say relevantly what we want to say.

More than anything else, I should think, they have discovered that no matter where we turn in our explorations of reality, every dimension of our knowledge is somehow, somewhere accredited by persons. Behind all our knowing stands the first personal pronoun *I*. Michael Polanyi has written with

7

impressive sensitivity on this theme, and to the knowledgeable reader my debt to the writings of Polanyi will be plain on nearly every page. My debt to Gabriel Marcel will be just as clear. His analysis of what it means to be a person is profoundly relevant to our understanding of Jesus. It centers upon the motif of wholeness. Words and acts are genuine, Marcel says, when we intend them to be so, when we undersign them with our signatures and claim them as our own. Words and acts are inseparable from the intention of the person who stands behind them and accredits them. I have taken this theme (which is also prominent in the writings of the later Wittgenstein) and applied it to the work and words of Jesus as a primary hermeneutic, or principle of interpretation. The sayings of Jesus and his acts of making men whole necessarily tell us a great deal about him as a person. More than that, they are signs through which we may intimate the presence of Jesus, and come to know him personally. If the book contains any polemic, it arises from my amazement at those New Testament critics who insist on the authenticity of Jesus' *word,* but who will have nothing to do with him as a person. I reject this attitude as a serious failure to understand what it means to be a person. To accredit someone's word and deeds is to accredit *him.* How this separation ever came about is a long story, but it goes back to Descartes and Kant, who were instrumental in splitting the world into subject against object. Western thought since their time has unfortunately come to admire third person language (it, him, them) to the neglect, and suspicion, of first and second person language (I, thou, we). But as Wittgenstein, Polanyi, Marcel, and a growing number of others have wisely reminded us, there never has been any radical separation in actual fact, because all our knowledge is at heart personal and metaphorical, even the knowledge of science. It is only when men have tried to explain what they thought they were about, that they have gone awry.

We are then in a position to know Jesus as a person through his words and acts. Because these are generally cast in the form of the kingdom of God metaphor, it serves as the medium through which we come to know him. He is the embodiment of the kingdom of God, the personalization of divine kingship. And here we come upon the importance of the concept of incarnation.

Merleau-Ponty and Marcel have described the *incarnate* nature of personal existence with great sensitivity. We are persons because we are embodied. That fact is of capital importance in understanding the significance of Jesus, for in him the Word becomes flesh, the grace of God becomes concretely personalized. Here again is a corrective to the idea that Christian faith is essentially a theology of the Word. No, it is a theology of the Word *become flesh*. The difference is a matter of the abstract (the third person model *it*) and the personal (first person *I*). For too long, in Bultmannian thought especially, the person of Jesus has been contracted out of New Testament studies, simply because the school has not had a really satisfactory concept of persons. At the same time, I make that criticism with deep appreciation of the important contributions the school has made to the existentialist interpretation of the New Testament. In our present study, for instance, Fuchs' discussion of Jesus' concept of time, and Käsemann's handling of the exorcisms have given me fresh inspiration. Yet it is a curious fact that none of these men seems genuinely interested in Jesus as a person. In his ideas, yes. And there is the real deficiency in the Bultmannian method: it suffers from abstraction, hence it is not thoroughly existentialist; for the existential is the concrete, and the concrete is personal. True, the school has always laid great emphasis upon personal consent and obedience to the fact that God is here at work in our present, but they have capitalized on the idea of pure word, pure immediacy with God, inwardness, and the kerygma (the proclamation of salvation) quite in isolation from the full concreteness of the world. This kind of existentialism is actually a negation rather than an affirmation of the world; it is closer to being a theology of disincarnation than of genuine concreteness in the world of persons.

The idea of concreteness and the process in which God's eternal love is realized in actual situations is the signal theme running through the writings of Charles Hartshorne. Although I will express some small cavil in the final chapter with his interpretation of death and resurrection, I am in debt to him for the creative way in which he sees God personally present in the richly concrete process of nature and history. God is not the timeless, changeless Being of classical metaphysics, but the creative God who is persuasively seeking to actualize his love in every dimension of the universe. Here is a tremendously exciting understanding of God, all the more so since it accords with the biblical idea of God as the One who seeks to bring wholeness into the world.

All these genuinely creative thinkers have contributed to my interpretation of Jesus and the kingdom, and I am grateful. There are others equally important—and that bears out the truth of Marcel's remark that every self is an interpersonal self: I am because I am with others. How true that is. Hence, my grateful thanks to those who have personally stimulated my thinking: Prof. Fred Carl Kuehner, who early in my academic career introduced me to the central importance of the kingdom of God in the ministry of Jesus; Prof. William Scott Noble, my former senior colleague, whose excellent teaching and patient liberalism smoothed the many rough edges of a teaching novice who had much to learn of that great period in theology; Prof. Eugene Peters, my colleague in philosophy and religion, whose thorough knowledge of Whitehead and Hartshorne and whose love of colloquy have greatly stimulated me; Prof. Dallas High, my second co-worker (blessed is he who is surrounded by good colleagues), who introduced me to Wittgenstein and Polanyi; my students in New Testament and Existentialism courses, who in daily give-and-take have left me a stronger and, I hope, a wiser man, with a deeper understanding of what genuine intersubjectivity means. And I am deeply indebted, perhaps most of all, to Prof. A. M. Hunter, a wise mentor and a warm friend, whose writings draw me back again and again, not for simple reason of their felicitous style, but because of their sensitive intimations of Jesus the person. He stands in a truly great tradition of interpreters who have never forgotten, in all their learned criticisms, that the Word became flesh.

For valued encouragement and financial assistance which made this book possible, I am grateful to the Fulbright Commission in Germany for a year of research at the University of Heidelberg in 1963-64, and to the administration of Hiram College for their liberal attitude toward grants and sabbaticals. I am also in debt to Dr. M. Jack Suggs, professor of New Testament in Brite College of the Bible, Texas Christian University, also on a research grant at Heidelberg the same year, whose helpful criticisms and encouragement in writing this book I have valued highly.

For treasured help in typing and proofreading, my grateful thanks are due my wife, my undergraduate assistant Robert Maurovich, Miss Judith Bosh, and Mrs. Olive White.

I express my gratitude to Miss Jeanette Kampen, copy editor for The Bethany Press, for her wise suggestions and expert help in bringing the book to completion.

ROYCE GORDON GRUENLER
HIRAM COLLEGE

Contents

PART I

JESUS, PERSONS,

AND THE

KINGDOM OF GOD

CHAPTER ONE

Personal Knowledge
and the
Witnesses to Jesus Christ

HOW DO WE in the twentieth century get to know a person whose life was lived in the past, when the only clues which lie at hand are the sketches and impressions left by others?

Our Western tradition places great emphasis upon persons and historical biography, yet we sometimes wonder how we can ever become acquainted with persons of the past. The answer lies in our power to "reembody" historical persons, not only in our imaginations but also in our intentionality, our language, and our acts: our whole persons, in short.

Accordingly, when we ponder the question of how we come to know a person of the past, we are awed by the active part we must play to relive that life which has already been lived. We repersonalize him from the witness he has left of himself, both in his writings (if there are any) and in the lives he has affected. And the lives he has touched for good or ill bear witness in their own language and their own acts to the quality of person he was. And so the search into that life that seems so far away goes on and on in a series of interpenetrations involving a host of witnesses, each of whom bears a portrait of the one we seek. Some are contradictory, and we learn to choose our sources with a scrutinizing eye, but as often as not we find them complementing one another, as each presents a facet of that life we seek to know.

History then—and can there be any doubt of it—is at deepest level the history of *persons,* not the history of ideas. That is a central point to put to good use in the study of Jesus and the kingdom of God. To be sure, ideas are important in any study of history, but ideas by themselves are abstractions. They merely point to someone who thought them, spoke them, and personally undersigned them. Ideas, like words and facts, are empty, totally empty, until someone vouches for them. Facts are always accredited facts; behind ideas there stands a person: and as for words, they are as true as the person who intends them to be true.[1]

What does this amount to? It comes to the insight that history, because it is always the history of persons, discloses its secrets only because we enter it on a personal level. As far as the study of Jesus and the kingdom of God is concerned, it means that we shall be most successful in knowing Jesus of Nazareth and the effect of his ministry when we approach his words and ways not as ends in themselves but rather as expressions of his inner intentionality. Here is the guide to fruitful historical knowing—the hermeneutic, if you will, that is to direct this study of the kingdom of God and the person of Jesus: words and works are inseparable from the person who speaks them and enacts them. Consideration of one involves the others. If, after some thought, I decide that I can undersign my name in good faith to a saying of Jesus which the evangelists report, I am not only accrediting the value of the saying but also I am subscribing to the integrity of the evangelists and their faithful witness—and I am saying something about Jesus himself. I am saying, "I believe that these words tell me something about the person of Jesus: I believe that he intended them to be true."

The same holds true for his acts. When I decide that I am willing to stake my reputation on the genuineness of a certain reported work of Jesus, I am not only accrediting the truth of the act but also I am attesting the intention of the witnesses, and I am saying that I believe Jesus intended to act in this manner because he was that kind of person.

The pattern is no different from our ordinary meeting of historical persons. There is no sacred hermeneutic and no profane historiography. All knowing is accredited knowing in which the knower is personally involved.

To the question of how it is even remotely possible to penetrate beyond all these witnesses, and beyond all personal involvement, to Jesus himself, a person might conclude that it is hopeless and give up the quest. The fact is, however, that there is no Jesus *in himself,* any more than there was ever that "thing-in-itself" Kant kept writing about, which was supposed to lie beyond all appearances. We must face up to the fact that there is no such entity as a thing-in-itself or a person-by-himself. That was the myth of Descartes, who thought that by closing himself inside a German oven he could systematically unrelate himself from everything except his interior thought.

That was a deception, but no more so than the popular idea that the historian's task is to penetrate beyond his witnesses to the historical person-in-himself. The truth of the matter is, a person is never a person in isolation. He *becomes* a person *in relation.* To be is not to be alone. To be is to be together: *esse est co-esse.* That means we interpenetrate one another so integrally that it is impossible for any person to think of himself without also calling to mind other persons who have participated in his life. Persons are copresent; they call one another into being simply by being there and calling forth potentialities which lie hidden and unrealized in all of us.

Existence, then, is participation. Reality *is* in the meeting. Persons place themselves at our disposal, open themselves up, as it were; we respond by placing ourselves at their disposal. In the meeting we call them into being, they call us into being, and together we come into being. Gabriel Marcel, who has written so penetratingly of these matters, reminds us that we are not subjects as a prior fact or point of departure, but become subjects as a conquest and a goal.[2]

Now this has the widest implications for our meeting historical persons. To know Jesus of Nazareth we go to those who knew him as an incarnate person. We apply criticism only where the gospel witnesses appear uncertain of their impressions, or where they describe the earlier Jesus as already raised to the level of the cosmic Christ. But mostly we are in their debt, and we go to them because they are inseparable from Jesus himself. They mediate him to us.

But if all we know of Jesus are the portraits of the evangelists, you may ask how we ever can hope to know Jesus himself. That is precisely the point. Jesus is not some entity-in-himself attainable only after we have stripped away the impressions of every witness. It is a great mistake to think in these Kantian terms. No, Jesus confronts us *in his witnesses* because the meaning of his person is inseparable from them.

It was these eyewitnesses, upon whose impressions the Gospels were based, who lived and talked with Jesus, who formed his audience and drew from him the creativity of his ministry. They participated in him and he in them.

Hence their witnesses to Jesus are aspects of the man himself. What we meet in the Gospels are "complementary aspections" of Jesus the subject which enable us to know him as a person. Many dimensions of his self are revealed to us there, sufficient for us to feel we know him and to know that he is copresent with us. The copresence we experience with him is not just a third-person knowing, but also a first-person participation. There is a unity established between us; we come into being; he ceases to be *him* and becomes *thou*.[3]

There lies the heart of historical knowing. Jesus is not a mere idea. If he were only a *him* he would be essentially absent from us. But he is not absent, because he is not a simple "idea." When we come to him, not with hostility but in the openness of fidelity, he becomes attached to our own personal reality; he continues to live in us in a mysterious kind of symbiosis which affects our thought, our intention, our language and acts.

Yet how do we participate in the person of Jesus when he is no longer incarnate? If it is my incarnate existence—my particular body in a particular place at a particular time—that creates the condition in which I can know and be known by other incarnate subjects, is Jesus not beyond our knowing? How is he in any sense incarnate?

He becomes incarnate again whenever we participate in the witnesses to his words and acts; and by participation we mean no mere intellectual exercise, but a participation of the self as unity: intention, word, act. Surely we no longer see Jesus walking about as his disciples once beheld him. We have not a clue as to his height, weight, features, or mannerisms. But these are never really crucial in getting to know a subject anyway, though it is true that we often judge a person solely on this superficial level.

There are deeper dimensions of personal knowledge. We know that Jesus had a body, a particular body people identi- fied with Jesus of Nazareth. We know that his body belonged to a particular geography in space, Palestine; and we know that it moved in a particular time, the first quarter of the first century of the Roman Empire.

That is where we begin, and it is a good beginning. The historical Jesus had his time, place, and particularity. But what shall we say of his uniqueness? What sort of person was he? (Notice, we are still speaking of him at a distance. Again we use the word *him,* which is a third-person model suggesting his absence.) In answer: we discover Jesus' uniqueness as a person when we are willing to accredit his witnesses and enter into their intersubjectivity with him.

When we do this, when we actually believe that certain words and acts are genuinely Jesus' own, we have already penetrated to the inner dimensions of his person.[4] This happens in ordinary day-to-day relationships with those we love and trust. We believe that their language and their works reveal them as they are and that our relationships with them are not hypocritical but genuine. Coming to know the Jesus of the Gospels begins with an understanding of what it means to know other persons whom we trust.

A central theme in this study of Jesus and the kingdom of God, a principle that has often been forgotten in modern thought, is: knowledge is always knowledge accredited by someone. Language that is meaningful is always language intentionally undersigned by responsible persons. Words must be backed up by appropriate action if they are to be believed and understood. In sum: words and acts are inseparable dimensions of persons who speak and perform them.

Now this is the depth at which Jesus ceases being a *him* and becomes a *thou*. In his works and words we meet him personally. Imaginatively we give him a body, we hear him speaking and see him healing the broken and exposing the hypocrisy of his critics. We are copresent with him at the profoundest level of his person—in his wholeness, in the unity of his intention, word and deed, which is the consummate uniqueness of his ministry. For the kingdom of God is the reign of God's grace and no mere abstraction, being particularized in Jesus' life and ministry. Jesus personifies the kingship of God, both in its healing and its judgment of men. He inaugurates the new time of God's appearing by setting before men a decision either to discover their unity in him and become whole again or to persist in arrogance and hypocrisy and lose sight of wholeness altogether.

Jesus' embodiment of the kingship of God is therefore a proclamation of wholeness against hypocrisy, agape against hubris. Every word and every act is an elaboration of this theme.

Now because this is true, Jesus becomes copresent with us to an unusual degree. He becomes an integral part of our reality, confronting *us* with the same call to decision and responsibility. Jesus has the unusual quality of being historical and historic at the same moment. We are drawn into his life situation, if only out of curiosity, and there we discover that he is speaking to us in our setting, laying before us the choice of wholeness or unwholeness.

That is why it is odd to find an existentialist such as Bultmann emphatically denying any relevance of Jesus to faith, beyond the fact that he was. Paul and John, he says, show no interest in the what and how of Jesus' history; they are unconcerned with his portrait, only with the cross, and that as an event, not as a piece of biography.[5] Therefore, Bultmann concludes, since the kerygma of the early Christian community is disinterested in Jesus' historicity beyond the *that,* Jesus does not personally mediate a new understanding of existence; his claims and promises do not extend beyond his earthly ministry. The new understanding of history occurs only in the kerygma of the church, which is not focused on the historical Jesus, but on the risen Lord.[6]

Here is a classic example of the modern scholar who has been deeply influenced by the Cartesian and Kantian thesis that there is a cleavage between the outer world and the inner world. By the application of this principle, the historical Jesus belongs to the outer realm of observable phenomena and the Christ of the kerygma belongs to the inner realm of faith. Careful reflection questions such a serious severing of knowledge. Is not every observable phenomenon in the "outer" dimension of history also accredited by personal faith?

It is odd that Bultmann can undersign a number of Jesus' personal characteristics, yet deny them any existential significance. He can say, for instance, that Jesus healed demoniacs, broke the sabbath law, abandoned ritual purifications, opposed Jewish legalism, fellowshiped with outcasts such as tax collectors and harlots, showed sympathy for women and children, forsook the ascetic life, called disciples, and formed a small company of followers about himself. In addition, he can say of his preaching that he certainly was conscious, indeed prophetically conscious, of having an authority and commission to proclaim the eschatological message that the kingdom of God was breaking in, and to present its demands and its invitation.[7] He believes that Jesus was no mere teacher or rabbi, but a prophet bearing an eschatological message, a man who as the bearer of God's word called for decision, the decision for salvation or judgment being made in terms of his own person. Jesus sees himself as an eschatological phenomenon, whose proclamation implies a Christology. His teaching is characterized by a directness, an immediacy, which places him above anything in contemporary Judaism.[8]

It would seem that if a biblical historian personally accredits the witnesses to Jesus to this extent, he has already confronted the intentionality of Jesus. To say so much about Jesus' uniqueness—is this not also to say that we meet him personally in these important aspects of his particularity? What more does Jesus need to do or say to convince us that he *intends* these kinds of acts and this sort of language? And if he stands behind his works and ways with intentional integrity, and if these words and deeds have a kerygmatic character and imply a Christology, as Bultmann admits,[9] how can we *not* conclude that Jesus intended his ministry to be kerygmatic and christological?

Yet Bultmann does not want to speak of Jesus in first- and second-person models. Jesus is always *him;* it is in his *word* that he is in the church's kerygma and confronts the hearer.[10] Here again is the third-person model which makes Jesus so distant—and absent. The Bultmannian language is full of abstractions: kerygma, word, event, eschatological occurrence. Even Christ seems an abstraction!

But abstractions will not do. Jesus rises into the kerygma, that is true. We can accept the idea that the "once" of the historical Jesus has risen into the "once-for-all" of the kerygma, in the sense that Jesus continues to be present in the decisions of every moment. But the kerygma does not swallow up Jesus, as it has in the word-theology. Rather, the kerygma is the personally accredited word of the disciples through whom we come to meet the historical Jesus again and again. Through their witness we are met by his wholeness, we hear his word of promise and judgment, and are moved to accept him or reject him.

What does Christian faith mean, if not this? The cross is the historical manifestation of suffering and tragedy in God, and of the evil response of men to a life of wholeness. The resurrection is the divine imprimatur upon the wholeness of the life Jesus lived, and a divine declaration that demonic forces, even death itself, are defeated in a life transparent to God and his paradisal will for creation.

The kerygma of the community is the proclamation that Jesus is of universal relevance. Wherever and whenever he is proclaimed, men are confronted by his concreteness, his humanness, and are brought into the presence of God.

"The Word became flesh and dwelt among us," says the writer of the Fourth Gospel. The Expression became flesh and bones. God eminently participated in a particular life in time and space. The kerygma is not a disincarnate return to abstract Word, but an appeal to participate in the wholeness of God, incarnate in Jesus.

Here lies the meaning of the kingdom of God. By itself, it is an abstraction. But Jesus uses it in such a way that the sensitive believer recognizes in it a veiled reference to Jesus himself, for its meaning is revealed in his words of reconciliation and his acts of healing.

How existential the language of the kingdom is! Our task is to listen to Jesus' witnesses with an ear sensitively attuned to the episodes which speak most elementally of personal existence. The parables are consummate examples of this primordial language of Jesus. The parable of the good Samaritan, as an instance, is as far from abstraction as one could imagine. God is never mentioned, though in the larger context of the lawyer's question he is the ground in which the encounter takes place. In this simple story of a man who risks his life and possessions to help a fellow being in distress, Jesus gets through to us directly on a personal level. We have to ask ourselves why this form of language communicates to us so directly.

This question allows an answer as profound as it is personal. The parable draws us into a situation we immediately recognize as our own. Its details may be first century, but no matter, we recognize the language. We are immediately engrossed in the episode, not as observers but as participants. Parables have a habit of doing that. Of all the forms of spoken language in Jesus' ministry, the parables are the most existential and primordial because they are concretely personal. They are alive. Jesus' preaching is always situational, never abstract.

Abstractions are slices out of the whole; Jesus involves us in the whole. He had an understanding of speaking which we have only recently begun to open up as a serious study in itself, the phenomenology of language. Maurice Merleau-Ponty, as an exponent of this phenomenology, writes of signs and speech and their power to draw us into the folds of "the immense fabric of language." When we abandon ourselves to the life, the movement, and eloquence of language, our thought passes through it, toward its deepest meaning. Signs are always indirect and allusive; they never express a meaning completely. They are punctuated by silence. Language does not have to say everything. A friend calls us on the telephone and his speech brings him to us as though he were wholly present.[11]

Now this is exactly the effect Jesus' language has on us. His speech is so rooted in the common meeting of persons that we are drawn into his situations as though they were our own. His words and acts become a medium of discovery, awakening us to what we tacitly know, but have seldom focused upon. They bring us out of our forgetfulness to the intersubjectivity of our common existence, and challenge us to decide what we shall do and who we shall become. The elemental nature of his language shocks us out of our forgetfulness and conveys us into the urgency of responsible action. This awakening from forgetfulness, Heidegger reminds us, is the root meaning of the ancient Greek word for truth, *aletheia.*[12]

All aspects of Jesus' ministry, his works of compassion as well as his words of grace and judgment, seem to have one point of focus: they awaken us to the urgency of becoming whole persons again in the world which is God's. Men have forgotten the source of authentic life, the creative presence of God, and they must be brought to unforgetfulness (which alone is truth) before they can become whole again.

This project is the burden of Jesus' teaching about the kingship of God.

It is not that God had never reigned as creative Lord prior to Jesus' coming, nor that Jesus brings about some change of heart in God by assuaging his anger and calling forth his mercy. That view of Jesus' ministry is as unworthy of God as it is of our knowledge of goodness. No, God has always from the very beginning been the personal and creative source of love and goodness. It is because of our hubris and casual insensitivity that we have fallen into forgetfulness of his presence. The burden of responsibility is ours: we have forgotten what it means to be persons within the Person who is God.

Accordingly, Jesus speaks to us in word and deed in such a way that he meets us directly at the deepest levels of personal experience—in concrete acts of loving others, judging evil, deciding for the way of goodness, taking the suffering of others upon ourselves, striving to be whole. All these we know but poorly, and in a forgetful way, so that we are unaware of him in whom we live.

The kingdom of God on the lips, in the works, in the life

of Jesus is God's way of calling us to unforgetfulness of him. It is a radical awakening from the sleep into which we have allowed ourselves to fall. Deep within we know God, but we have suppressed him into the remote recesses of our unconscious. All we have left is a tacit awareness of God.

Jesus announces that God has made a creative passage into the world of sleeping men. In him God has become flesh and bones in order that we may see his life as the very embodiment of God's kingly rule in the world. Origen once said that Jesus is himself the kingdom, *autobasileia*. There is much truth in that.

Not that one human life can embody the inexhaustible creativity of God. No single person can do that. But in one important respect Jesus *is* the kingship of God. We see it in the creative fidelity of his life. By fidelity we mean that Jesus lived consummately in God's creative presence. His life was eminently whole in the degree to which he penetrated and was penetrated by God. In him the Word became flesh. The life Jesus lived was an expression of the copresence of the divine and the human. And when men acknowledge him as that expression, the kerygma comes into being, and Jesus has then risen to become the Lord, Christ and Savior of every man.

Jesus was not the first expression of God's grace toward men, nor the last. No Christian needs to say that. God has always and everywhere been the creative force of sociality, for existence is essentially social, and wherever it is realized in love and justice God is present in the midst. Certainly he was present in the great spiritual processes of the Axial Period, as Jaspers calls it,[13] centering about the sixth century B.C., when the inexhaustible activity of God made a creative passage in the thoughts and works of sensitive men. At that time, nearly six hundred years before Christ, Confucius and Lao-tzu appeared in China, and with them a host of Chinese schools of philosophy. In India the Upanishads and the Bhagavad-Gita were written by the followers of Hinduism;

and there Gautama Buddha came to teach a simpler way of curing the soul-sorrow of man. In Iran, Zarathustra taught his view of a world struggling with good and evil. In Palestine, the great prophets of Israel and Judah came preaching their message of Yahweh's steadfast love and justice, with a call to forsake idolatry and social injustice. And in Greece there appeared the great bard Homer, the pre-Socratic philosophers, Plato and Aristotle, and the tragedians Aeschylus, Sophocles, and Euripides. In three great civilizations—China, India, and the West—there was a strange movement of the spirit which we can only acknowledge as an interpenetration of divine-human creativity.

In the history of Israel itself, the Old Testament people thought of God's activity in time. They viewed the fulfillment of time, or the end, not as rectilinear movement, but as nodal or punctiliar. Time took on meaning because it was located around significant events or persons. Gerhard von Rad develops this theme with great understanding[14] by showing how the whole life of Israel moved about the remembering of particular events in the religious festivals. The exodus events were remembered at Passover; in remembrances like these, history took on meaning because God had acted at certain times and places. Israel's understanding of history was punctiliar: it was the particularity of occasions which located the Jewish people and gave them their identity.

The prophetic movement in the Axial Period of the eighth to sixth centuries B.C. brought to light new dimensions of God's activity. He was now experienced as the Lord who works as equally in the present as in the past, and who allows his people promise of his redemptive activity in the future. This new understanding of God's activity gave rise to the eschatological view of history which is so much a part of Jesus' understanding of time. The prophets looked backward and forward, backward to God's great redemptive activity in the past, and forward to analogous activity in the future.

They did not look forward to the end of time and history as such, but to a new entrance into the promised land, as in Hosea; to a new David and a new Zion, as in Isaiah; to a new covenant, as in Jeremiah; and to a new exodus, as in the Second Isaiah. They anticipated a new time and a new history.

The prophets did not forget the past, but their faith is given a forward thrust because the present stands in tension with the future promise and judgment of God. Worship of Yahweh and intention toward one's neighbor have an ultimate significance about them, because the promise and judgment which the future holds are decided upon in the present. The intensity of authentic speech and acts in the here and now is heightened by anticipation of the yet to come. This is an existentialist understanding of God and persons in time and space. Every moment is an ultimate moment because a man literally exists in three dimensions of God's creative activity: past, present, and future. The believer exists in time, and he "stands outside of himself" (ex-ists) when he recalls the past, anticipates the future, and speaks and acts in the now in full view of that which was and that which is to come.

After the sixth century B.C., the kingdom of God was understood in this way: Yahweh was worshiped as the eternal king (see Exod. 15:18; Ps. 145:11 ff.), but his kingship was allied with an expectation of his future kingly activity (Mic. 2:12 f.; 4:1-7; Isa. 24:21-23; 33:22; 52:7-10; Zeph. 3:14-20; Obad. 21). The reign of God (which is the primary meaning of the Hebrew *malkuth shamayim*) was to be experienced in a decisive creative occasion when God would disclose himself as the saving king of his people.

It would be more in keeping with our thesis that history is the history of persons if we were to make use of C. K. Barrett's suggestion that God's creative activity in history is to be identified with representative *persons* in the history of salvation. Paul understood that history gathers at specific nodal points which are represented by outstanding figures. These persons incorporate the human race, or parts of it, and represent their fellowmen before God. The five nodal representatives of biblical history are Adam, Abraham, Moses, Christ, and "The Man to Come."[15]

The creative occasion in which the kingly activity of God breaks through with new universal significance, is Jesus Christ. It is in Jesus that we discover a life that is luminous to the very structures of existence. The wholeness of personal existence is personified in his intentionality, his language, his works, so that in knowing him we come to know the ways and works of God, and the interrelation of God and men. So representative and so universally significant is Jesus of Nazareth, that God raised him into the kerygma of cosmic significance. "To proclaim God's kingly activity in the new time, proclaim Jesus Christ." That is the belief of those who come to know that man in whom God was incarnate. For it was such a one who flashed upon the world a personal wholeness which added something once for all. In this epochal occasion, in the microcosmic figure inclusive of the whole universe, God made a new Expression of what all men know (but have forgotten) that he might evoke in us an intuitive expression of response.

READINGS ON CHAPTER ONE

Barrett, C. K. *From First Adam to Last: A Study in Pauline Theology.* New York: Charles Scribner's Sons, 1962.

Braaten, Carl E., and Harrisville, Roy A. (eds. and trans.). *The Historical Jesus and the Kerygmatic Christ: Essays on the New Quest of the Historical Jesus.* New York: Abingdon Press, 1964.

Bultmann, Rudolf. *Jesus and the Word.* Translated by L. P. Smith and E. H. Lantero. London: Fontana Books, 1958.

――――. *Theology of the New Testament,* Vol. I. Translated by K. Grobel. London: SCM Press, 1952.

Hartshorne, Charles. *The Logic of Perfection and Other Essays in Neoclassical Metaphysics.* La Salle, Ill.: Open Court Publishing Co., 1962.

Harvey, Van A. *The Historian and the Believer.* New York: The Macmillan Company, 1966.

Heidegger, Martin. *Being and Time.* Translated by J. Macquarrie and E. Robinson. New York: Harper & Row, 1962.

Heschel, Abraham J. *The Prophets.* New York: Harper & Row, 1962.

Jaspers, Karl. *The Origin and Goal of History.* New Haven: Yale University Press, 1953.

Marcel, Gabriel. *Creative Fidelity.* Translated by Robert Rosthal. New York: Noonday Press, 1964.

Merleau-Ponty, Maurice. *Signs.* Translated by R. C. McCleary. Evanston: Northwestern University Press, 1964.

Perrin, Norman. *The Kingdom of God in the Teaching of Jesus.* London: SCM Press, 1963.

Peters, Eugene H. *The Creative Advance.* St. Louis: The Bethany Press, 1966.

Polanyi, Michael. *Personal Knowledge: Towards a Post-Critical Philosophy.* Harper Torchbooks; New York: Harper & Row, 1964.

————. *The Tacit Dimension.* New York: Doubleday, 1966.

von Rad, Gerhard. *Old Testament Theology,* Vols. I & II. Translated by D. M. G. Stalker. New York: Harper & Row, 1962 & 1965.

Ricoeur, Paul. *Fallible Man: Philosophy of the Will.* Translated by Charles Kelbley. Henry Regnery Company, 1965.

CHAPTER TWO

The
Parabolic Language
of Jesus

HISTORY has many dimensions. It is comprised of the factual-
ness of the past; it possesses the quality of futurity, opening
up to us all sorts of possibilities to be grasped; and it meets
us in the present, where we relive the past and anticipate the
future. Each facet of history has its inner and outer dimensions as well, and neither can work without the other.

Jesus employs these many facets of experience in his parables. He always describes a "public" situation (the outer
dimension of history) which enables us to get hold of the
setting in an imaginative way, then he draws us into the inner
dimension where we are personally involved in the action of
the story. He moves us from the position of observers, looking
at public action, to the position of participants, where we are
faced with the responsibility to decide and act.

Some of his parables emphasize that the reign of God has
already come in his ministry, others place an accent on the
process of growth, and still others stress a future judgment
and fulfillment. Yet all are inseparably tied together. We
would expect that, for the reign of God is a new time (*kairos*)
which brings with it a new understanding of personal existence, experienced in all the rich and full dimensions of time
itself.

Come, coming, yet to come—these are the facets of the kingdom. Yet Jesus' primary focus of time is always the present. In each parable he lays before us our responsibility to decide for the kingdom of God which is here to be entered. He allows us, as he did his disciples, to make up our own minds about its precise manner of coming. Sometimes it comes catastrophically, as it did in the persecution of the early church and during the suffering of the last war; at other times, it comes quietly like the seed growing mysteriously. But always, the divine creativity which Jesus personifies calls us to personal commitment. We are to become sensitive to its presence everywhere and at every moment.

To come to know the intention of Jesus through his understanding of time and God's reign among men is the purpose that guides this study. Some attention needs to be given at this point to the interpretation of the parables, though it is not necessary to rehearse the long history of this search.

First of all, a parable is not an allegorical treasury, as Origen supposed. Generally it has one central thrust. Jülicher brought that fact to light at the turn of the century, and we are grateful to be relieved of the quest for hidden meanings which characterized earlier generations.[1] On the other hand, we must not let a happy theory bind us unpleasantly, for there are a few parables that invite a limited allegorical treatment. Second, Jesus' parables are always situational. They are not universal moral preachments (Jülicher went wrong here). Universal maxims are abstracts of real life, while the parables set up concrete situations. Jesus leads us into situations we recognize as our own; and meeting us where we are, he draws us into the setting of his personal ministry.

Finally, the metaphors of Jesus illustrate his ability to employ the most direct forms of spoken language. They are as primordial as the meeting between Nathan and David (2 Sam. 12:1-15) where David is drawn into the parable of the poor man and his lamb. As David discovers, the parable is an

34

existential communication involving the very values of his life. Similarly, the parables of Jesus draw us into live situations and call our own values to a reckoning.[2]

Now, because metaphorical language is so elemental and direct, it is a pity that Mark has suggested just the opposite. He would have us believe that Jesus purposely used the parables to hide God's truth from his people. Only the disciples were given privileged access to their meaning (Mark 4:11-12): "To you has been given the secret of the kingdom of God, but for those outside everything is in parables; so that they may indeed see but not perceive, and may indeed hear but not understand; lest they should turn again, and be forgiven."

It is not an easy matter to unravel Mark's interpretation. There are probably two main reasons that led him to his conclusion. The first is Jesus' somewhat elusive attitude toward his personal role as Messiah. This naturally gave rise to some questioning among his disciples as to what manner of man he was. Perhaps it was more his unorthodox ministry that raised the query, betraying the insensitivity of his disciples to his elemental life.

The disciples are usually described in a pejorative manner in the Gospels. They seldom see the point, they argue with Jesus, they are hardhearted and hardheaded. Their leader, Peter, comes off worst of all. This suggests an underlying motif: Jesus' ministry is so profoundly personal that even his disciples fail to divine its deepest meaning, in spite of private instruction. Perhaps this mystery-motif reflects the failure of the people generally to respond to Jesus. The trouble with Mark's solution, however, is that it places the major responsibility on Jesus' method of instruction rather than upon the inability of his listeners to hear clearly a simple, existential language in the long tradition of the great prophets of Israel.

We suspect that Mark has improperly used a Targum variation of Isaiah 6:9 f., associated it with the parables, and interpreted it as a saying of purpose rather than result. Isaiah's ministry was never intended to veil the message of God any more than Jesus' own. It did turn out to have that effect, not because his preaching was unclear but because his people were unwilling to put it responsibly into action. It was their responsibility, not the fault of the message.

In a similar way, Jesus' ministry is directed to the heart, ears, and eyes of his people, not purposely to becloud them but to awaken them to their responsibility to decide for or against God. The parables are purposely chosen to illustrate the presence of divine grace, not to obscure it. Jeremias has suggested that Mark has inserted the word "parables" into a passage which does not really allow the word. He has interpreted the Aramaic word *mathla* as "parable" when a better rendering is "riddle" or "dark saying."[3] If we combine this correction with T. W. Manson's suggestion that the "so that" of verse 12 should be rendered "who" (the Aramaic *de* is flexible),[4] we come off with a translation far removed from Mark's:

> To you has been given the secret of the kingdom of God, but everything is in riddles for those outside who indeed see but do not perceive, who indeed hear but do not understand, unless they should turn again and be forgiven.

A look at the parables themselves is enough to assure us that we have read Mark's intention correctly. They are direct communications in the best sense, confronting us with the momentous news of God's grace. It is true that the parables here and there reflect the flexibility with which members of the early church adapted the sayings of Jesus to their own situations; but in one sense this is a good thing because it shows that Jesus had made his point about the relevance of the gospel to concrete situations. Yet it sometimes makes the recovery of the original setting difficult. Sound judgment is needed today in distinguishing the setting of the church from Jesus' own, where there is compelling reason. But this is not the exact science form criticism once hoped it would be. It is well to heed the word of Robert Grant that in general a sharp separation between the life settings of Jesus and the church is mistaken, because we are simply ignorant of the exact differences between the two. The genuineness of a saying cannot be determined alone on an external analysis of the stages of tradition, because every analysis is governed by presuppositions regarding the general trustworthiness of the records and sayings.[5]

A guiding assumption in this study of the parables is that a critical posture should always be second to that of faith. That is Polanyi's thesis regarding the art of knowing in general, and the point is well taken in biblical studies.

The extreme criticism in some quarters of New Testament interpretation has been guided by the principle of doubt: no saying of Jesus is to be accredited unless we are compelled to accept it. The faith required in this assumption is considerable, and it has led us about as far as we can go in the direction of the doubt lined out by the thinkers of the seventeenth century.

We choose to give pride of place to the general reliability of the gospel witnesses, doubting authenticity only when compelled by obvious inconsistency in the witnesses, as in Mark's interpretation of the parables, for example. Our guiding principle is, "Innocent until proven guilty," not the other way round.

With this in mind, we turn to the parables themselves.

The metaphors of Jesus have one theme in common: they are all charged with the excitement of a new event. God has made a creative passage into the world of men in the person of Jesus. It is the divine reign of compassion and justice, the kingdom of God. These are not new themes, and Jesus does not pretend that they are. The Old Testament is full of the expectation that God's kingdom will some day come in universal splendor.

But the creative disclosure which God is making is new in this sense: the eternal nature of God, his love and goodness, now finds new expression in the concreteness of a life that is lived. Jesus of Nazareth is bringing the new era of God's kingdom in his words, his deeds, his intention—his life. He embodies the kingdom; he is *autobasileia.*

According to Mark, the new period is inaugurated as Jesus begins his ministry in Galilee: "The momentous time (*kairos*) has come to fulfillment. The reign of God is upon you (*ēggiken*). Change your lives and believe in the good news" (Mark 1:15, author's translation).

Here, then, is the first indication of the nature of the reign of God. It is God's presence here and now, inaugurated in a new way through the life of this man. Since we come to know others because they are incarnate, and participate in the world because we can relate it to our persons, is this not a "divine passage"—a breakthrough—that God now finds a life so sensitive to his presence that he can embody himself in that life, and become incarnate in the world? The divine creativity of the new era is that God is now personally embodied. The human metaphors of the Old Testament are fulfilled in Jesus who becomes the Divine Metaphor.

"Becomes" is the proper word, for a person is never fully disclosed in any frame of his life, not only because he is an inexhaustible and many-dimensional subject but also because he is always becoming more himself in each successive moment. That is why the reign of God which Jesus personifies has come, comes, and is yet to come at every stage of his ministry. To be a person is to have a body in a certain place at a certain time, hence the time-liness and world-liness of the reign of God which Jesus embodies. He *is* and *becomes* the kingdom.

We may enter the parables, then, in the three dimensions of personal existence. They describe a situation which has come, or better, which has begun to come; a situation in which we now stand; and a possibility now to be grasped in the face of a situation yet to come. The dimensions of time never stand entirely apart, but form a unity. It is simply that one facet is now emphasized, then another. The parables are grouped here three-dimensionally only for convenience.

Parables of Realization

1. The reign of God has come, the time is fulfilled. This study begins not as might be expected with the longer and more involved parables but with the "terse similes" that Jesus employed to proclaim the momentous coming of the new age in his ministry. It is no accident that Jesus uses quick and to-the-mark illustrations to bring his message home at the start, as the Old Testament prophets had done centuries before. An exciting message makes a bearer breathless, like the ancient runner who brings good news.

a. The bridegroom is here, Jesus says, and that is why his disciples are not fasting, unlike the followers of John the Baptist who stand between the old and the new and are not yet aware that this is the time to celebrate God's creative ingress into human affairs (Mark 2:18-20). The marriage festivities are upon us, the wedding guest can hardly fast when the bridegroom is present for his marriage. The thrust of this metaphor is obvious. The Old Testament is replete with metaphors of marriage in which Yahweh is the bridegroom and Israel the bride. And though the prophets' message often judges the faithless wife who was betrothed in her youth but now has promiscuously followed other husbands, idols, and false gods, its primary imagery is extremely powerful. To know God is not just a matter of conceptualizing him in the intellect, though reason plays its role in any authentic relationship, but of knowing him as a wife knows her husband. It involves the commitment of a whole person to another, where nothing is held back. The intimacy of love which marks a marriage is best described as creative fidelity, to borrow Gabriel Marcel's expression. The lover passes beyond the distant third person models of *him* and *her* to the intimacies of *thou* and the mystery of *we*.

That is why the metaphor of the bridegroom is a profoundly moving image, brief as it is, for it not only links us to the great metaphorical tradition of the Old Testament but draws us into an experience we recognize as our own. While the metaphor of marriage is only an intimation of the inexhaustibly rich experience of knowing God, it is unquestionably a sign of great effectiveness.

The fact that the Old Testament people thought of themselves as the bride of Yahweh, betrothed to him at the beginning of their history, means that God does not come as the bridegroom for the first time in Jesus of Nazareth. But he does come in a new way which betokens the new era; he comes incarnate in a human life that personally manifests the intimate love of God.

The metaphor is especially appropriate because it introduces us to Jesus' ministry and the kingdom of God. The fact that his disciples do not fast can have but one meaning: the reign of God "has come upon" the world. The promised kingdom was always associated in the Jewish hope with a great messianic banquet, and now its arrival is expressed in the joyful feasting of the disciples.

Jesus accordingly stands out as the central figure in the divine reign which has now come upon the world in his person. Assuming the genuineness of this saying, we have to conclude that it reflects his inner intentionality. He is conscious of his role as the inaugurator of the new time. He is aware of his mission. Each reader will have to decide whether he interprets his mission as messianic or not, though it seems difficult to separate the mission from a messianic consciousness.

One other point begs hearing. Jesus' saying is evoked by the critical remarks of his opponents who have other messianic ideas. Why are the disciples of Jesus not fasting like the disciples of John? The implication is that Jesus and his followers are irreligious. Jesus' answer not only distinguishes him from the old era but also immediately engages him in conflict with the "misunderstanders" who pursue him all the way to his death. This bears out a fundamental truth about the reign of God: wherever it appears, it sets itself against evil, ignorance, and forgetfulness. Jesus' ministry is perforce a ministry of conflict. The fight against evil emerges at the start and continues to the end.

b. Whether or not the twin parables of the patch and the wineskins which follow (Mark 2:21 f.) are Jesus' own or reflect the early church's conflict with Judaism, they contrast the old with the new. The point is, something has happened: The new time has begun. The metaphor of wine is a banquet image which is used by the writer of the Fourth Gospel to recount the incident of the wedding at Cana (John 2:1-11—could it be that the story has a similar setting to the bridegroom saying in Mark?). And of course the chalice of wine figures importantly at the Last Supper in the upper room, where it symbolizes not only the new age of God's visitation but also his visitation in the life of a person. The wine is the blood of his life lived in love for the world.

c. The theme of coming and controversy appears again in the tremendous saying of Jesus, "Those who are well have no need of a physician, but those who are sick; I came not to call the righteous, but sinners" (Mark 2:17 and para.). There is great irony here, as Jesus opposes the hypocritical criticism of the religionists who object to his associating with sinners and tax collectors. With ironic humor he calls them "righteous," but it is a serious humor exposing their insensitivity to suffering and evil. Here again the new is contrasted with the old. The physician is concerned for the ill; they are not. But even more important is Jesus' identification with the healing physician. He uses the personal pronoun *I*: "I came. . . ." We could hardly ask for a clearer word on Jesus' understanding of his mission.

The bridegroom and physician metaphors set the tone for his ministry. He personifies the new era; he calls for joyous feasting; and he exemplifies sensitive compassion for the sick and unrighteous as well as vigorous opposition to bad faith.

d. Sensitivity to suffering and opposition to evil are central in Jesus' warfare against the demonic realm.

Many of us find it hard to take these sayings as literally as our forefathers did, but metaphorically they bear a tremendous impact. The battle against disease and evil-possession is described by Jesus (again rebutting the charges of his opponents) as a binding of the strong man Satan whose house he then enters in order to despoil his goods (Mark 3:27 and para.). The invasion of the demonic realm has already begun in his ministry of healing: "But if it is by the finger [Matt.: "Spirit"] of God that I cast out demons, then the kingdom of God has come upon you" (Luke 11:20; Matt. 12:28, Q). The verb *ephthasen* emphatically reveals Jesus' intention to say that the reign of God has come in his ministry.

These metaphors, which proclaim the kingdom's arrival, are personal and convincing. Jesus is the bridegroom, the physician, the plunderer of evil. The next few sets of metaphors are more situational, and even more elemental in their power to involve us personally.

2. The reign of God has come, bringing warning, exhortation and forgiveness.

a. The parable of the two debtors is embedded in the story of the woman with the ointment (Luke 7:36-50). It is a setting within a setting. The woman is a sinner of the city who finds her way to Simon the Pharisee's house where Jesus is dining.

There, in tearful repentance she washes his feet with her tears, wipes them with her hair, kisses and anoints them with an alabaster flask of ointment which she has brought with her. Simon is disgusted. Jesus should know better. Why does he not remonstrate with this well-known strumpet? Instead, Jesus remonstrates with Simon the Pharisee.

The conflict is typical of the other encounters in which Jesus sets himself against hypocrisy. Simon claims to be religious, but lacks wholeness and fidelity. Repeatedly Jesus' own words reveal his intentional fidelity. He tries to elicit this wholeness in others. Simon shows how human relations break down when persons fail to stand behind pious utterances with appropriate public behavior. But the woman, who knows her emptiness, has been called back into being by the wholeness of Jesus.

In the parable within the story, Simon turns out to be the less sensitive debtor who has had less forgiven, while the woman loves more because her sins are greater. The woman is grateful for the self-renewal she has found in Jesus. But Simon turns out to be the greater sinner because he is insensitive to what has happened in the profound experience of reconciliation. He is so shackled by a religious system which judges others at a distance that he never recognizes her as a *thou,* and so he is unable to participate with her in the most personal realm of *we.* Jesus incarnates God's healing compassion by doing just that. Simon does not see the reign of God which is present in his very house. The woman does. She knows the meaning of grace.

b. A similar contrast is made in the parable of the two sons (Matt. 21:28-32). Again the setting is "in conflict." Jesus contrasts the nominal obedience of the scribes and Pharisees with the tax collectors and harlots. These sinners may have been disobedient, like the first son who refused to go and work in the father's vineyard. But they have repented and gone to serve in the vineyard that is God's kingdom. The leaders of religion, however, promise to work but do not keep their word. What they do condemns what they say: "They preach, but do not practice" (Matt. 23:3). But authentic man is a unity, a gestalt, whose behavior is integral to his intention. Here the theme of personal fidelity stands out again. Gabriel Marcel makes the same point when he says that an action I am unwilling to undersign with my signature as if to say, "It is mine, I am responsible for it," is a mere gesture, not an act at all. Jesus is accusing his critics of playacting. They are only gesturing, playing at religion.

The parables of the two debtors and the two sons use a technique of existential "entrapment" which carries us along in a situation of great interest. We are asked to render a verdict, which we are quick to do since it is someone else's predicament, not ours. Too late, we discover that the parable is about us. Nathan used the same parabolic technique to awaken David to his responsibility, as we have already seen (2 Sam. 12:1-7).

c. Entrapment is also the purpose of the parable of the Pharisee and the publican (Luke 18:9-14). The conflict is clear in the first sentence. Jesus tells the parable "to some who trusted in themselves that they were righteous and despised others." Hubris is double-edged in its destructiveness. It is arrogant before transcendence and contemptuous of men. Simon the Pharisee was arrogant toward Jesus and contemptuous of the woman. Here the theme is the same. Like the others, the parable stresses the present reality of divine grace and the honest openness required to experience it. It is a story of forgiveness, warning and exhortation. The Pharisee is arrogant before God and contemptuous of the publican. He is insensitive to the actual presence of God and insensitive to the publican as a person. The publican is conscious of his inadequacy, and thus receptive to reconciliation. The scene is so beautifully described that we can re-create it in our imagination, or better, we recognize it as our own, letting it prod us

44

to a personal response that encompasses our whole selves, bodies as well as minds, acts and words as well as thoughts. It is only because God's reconciling reign is present that this can be so.

d. The twin parabolic sayings of the lost sheep and the lost coin (Luke 15:3-6, 8-9) were likely coined by Jesus to answer opponents who resisted his attitude toward the socially undesirable. Here the search and the joy of discovery are, interestingly, all on the part of the searcher. These short parables are preeminently parables of grace. The primary note is that God is seeking men as intensely as a shepherd seeks a lamb or as a woman seeks a coin from a dowry of coins singularly precious to her. Jesus is asking his critics why they should resent his concern for the lost of the world when God takes such joy in finding his own lost possessions.

e. The parable of the prodigal son (Luke 15:11-32) is a classic, and Luke knowingly places it here because it shares the note of lostness-discovery as well as the present accessibility of grace. It is the third in his trilogy on this basic theme. It has two major points and allows of some allegorical interpretation. God is the father, the publicans and sinners are the prodigal, and the scribes and Pharisees the elder brother. Once more we recognize the polemic setting of the parable as a true reflection of the resistance Jesus encountered in his ministry of compassion. Against the attitude of the elder son, he justifies his ministry of forgiveness. The first point of the story centers upon the intention of the prodigal who is at first egocentric, then repentant, and finally reconciled. But central attention is given to the father who waits with paternal care for the lost son to return (there is no predestinarian compulsion; the son must make the decision himself). Helmut Thielicke has wisely called this the parable of the waiting father.[6]

The final altercation between father and elder son comes off in an admirably irenic spirit, for Jesus' intention (he represents the father; the elder son, the scribes and Pharisees) is to win them over, not win over them. The parable is a remarkable statement of God's creative ministry of grace in Jesus to the lost. Like the other parables it refers to one situation in order to illuminate another. That is why the parables are so lively. By relating a life-setting they enlighten our own, warning us, exhorting us, and opening up to us the possibilities of grace.

3. The kingdom of God has come: the importance of decision, risk, and discipleship. The parables in this group underscore the urgency of risking the values of life for the treasure of the kingdom which is upon us.

a. This is succinctly illustrated in the twin parables of the hidden treasure and the costly pearl (Matt: 13:44-46). These are especially important sayings because they explicitly compare the kingdom of heaven (Matthew's synonym for the kingdom of God) to priceless treasures now obtainable. The reign of God is a treasury of new life and can be secured by the person who is willing to risk the loss of lesser values. Indeed, once he finds the kingdom, other values pale, and he gladly gives them up. In the first parable, that of the hidden treasure, a farmer accidentally strikes against something while digging in a field, and discovering that it is a hidden treasure, in joyous haste he sells all he has to secure it. In the second, the pearl merchant who has been looking all his life for a find like this, sells everything to get it.

The reign of God is here, these parables say. It is an ultimate value outclassing all others. Risk everything to obtain it.

Ernst Fuchs pays considerable attention to the concept of time which is implicit in these parables. Whether Jesus is speaking of the kingdom that has come and is now an open possibility, or is quietly and invisibly in process of coming, or is yet to come in fuller dimension, his appeal is always concrete. The kingdom is always a possibility to be grasped in every life situation. It is good news to know that the treasure of God's creative presence is always at hand, ready to reconcile and renew and create anew if we embrace it and allow it to embrace us.[7]

b. Where the parables of the hidden treasure and the pearl of great price compare the valuable with the invaluable, another set focuses upon the cost to the purchaser. The parables of the tower builder and the warring king (Luke 14:28-30, 31-32) illustrate what total commitment means, warning us of the risks and responsibilities of discipleship. Before a man begins to build a tower (the silo of a farm?), he had better consult his finances lest he run out of money before he finishes.

In a different setting, the same consideration is imperative. Here a king stands to lose a kingdom if he throws his men against an army twice the size. So he compromises and sues for peace.

We cannot be sure whether Jesus tied the saying in verse 33 to the two parables, but it brings the sense of the passage before us. It is a great risk for us to become disciples; it requires our whole persons. Are we up to it? Yet obviously, we can only be asked to assert our capabilities when a role is a real possibility. Jesus' repeated invitations and warnings of the cost of discipleship offer evidence of the reality of God's new time, which is the time of the kingdom. The kingdom *is* real; it is a gift to be chosen. Are we willing to risk the choice and accept the responsibilities that accompany the gift?

c. But one must make up his mind and not dally. The "weighing" sayings should be compared with Luke 9:57-62; Matthew 8:19-22, Q, where Jesus confronts the man who swears he will follow him wherever he goes, warning him not to flirt with time but to follow straightway and "go and proclaim the kingdom of God." While this man first wants to bury his father, a second asks to bid his family farewell, but Jesus replies, "No one who puts his hand to the plow and looks back is fit for the kingdom of God" (Luke 9:62). Even Elijah allows his successor Elisha to say his good-byes and hold a final banquet (1 Kings 19:19-21), but Jesus' call to discipleship will allow no delay. Hyperbole, perhaps, but it bears out the existential truth that an individual does not become a genuine person until he commits his whole life to responsible action. He cannot waste time; he must act.

d. The trouble with these men is that like so many they fail to take seriously the new passage of God's reign in Jesus' ministry. They are like the children in the parable of the children in the marketplace (Luke 7:31-35; Matt. 11:16-19, Q). This parable caricatures the immaturity of a generation that plays at games while their world is falling to pieces. Like frivolous children who play first at dancing, then at funeral, they are never serious enough to consider the time which Jesus brings. They only complain, shifting criticism to John the Baptist, whom they denounce as demonically austere, and to Jesus whom they write off as "a glutton and a drunkard, a friend of tax collectors and sinners."

e. If the word demonic is appropriate to any, it must apply to these petulant critics who are too insensitive to see how the concept of love is magnificently unfolded in new dimensions by Jesus' compassion for the outcasts. Perhaps the enigmatic parable of the empty house (Luke 11:24-26; Matt. 12:43-45, Q) may be read as a commentary on Luke 11:20—Jesus' invasion of demonic evil will have lasting effect only if his disenslaved people resolve to follow responsibly and live out their cleansing within the reign of God. If they fail to respond to the cleansing Jesus brings, they will be like the man who is healed of a demonic spirit but leaves the "house" of his life empty, whereupon the unclean spirit returns with seven others, "and the last state of that man becomes worse than the first."

f. The conflict between Jesus' compassion to all and the religionists' refusal to recognize him, is told again in a remarkable story of grace, the parable of the laborers in the vineyard (Matt. 20:1-16). Like the parable of the prodigal son, where the center of interest is God the waiting Father, the central figure of this parable is the owner of the vineyard.

The reign of God is not purchased by the number of hours we have worked. It is a gift bestowed by God. That is bad economics, but the parable has nothing to do with ordinary salaries and rewards. It presents an existential situation of the eleventh hour (Jesus' ministry) when those who have never before been hired to work (the publicans and sinners) are given the same wage (the gift of renewal in the kingdom of God), over the loud objections of those who have been working in the vineyard since the start of the day.

These are allegorical touches, but the issue is clear enough: the parable rebukes the resentful, the ones who resent the equal treatment given by the owner of the vineyard. The creative passage God is now making in Jesus eminently expresses his grace toward all. Jesus is saying that in the way of divine grace the first and the last share alike. The idea that "We were here first" has no claim upon God, for God is the ever-present ground of genuine existence for all men, not for just a favored few.

This parable, incidentally, is one that Jülicher judges inauthentic because of its allegorical touches. That only illustrates how harnessed the single-point theory can be. In fact, the metaphor shares the theme of all the others: divine grace is now disclosed in the eleventh hour of Jesus' new time as a gift to all men, and this disclosure rebukes the cult of particularism.

Jesus' ministry manifests the tremendous fact—and it is truly breathtaking in the history of religions—that in the marketplace of men every person is hired to labor in the vineyard of God. The wages are qualitative; they cannot be quantitatively measured. The equality of men in the economy of grace is basic to Jesus' understanding of existence, and underlies the apostolic teaching of the unity of Jew and Greek, slave and free, male and female in Christ Jesus (Gal. 3:28).

g. In all these parables we are struck by the worldliness of the settings. They are drawn from ordinary life, not from theological doctrines. Here is existential language, concrete and relevant, that overcomes the disastrous distinction between the sacred and the secular by which some would divide our world down the center. Jesus affirms the fundamental goodness of the world by drawing his illustrations from worldly settings. His language reiterates the words of Genesis 1, "And God saw that it was good." For Jesus everything is sacred. That is why genuinely human acts manifest the grace of God and serve as univocal models of his continual creativity.

The parable of the good Samaritan (Luke 10:29-37) exemplifies the force of the "worldly" example. True, there are considerable critical questions regarding the context in which Luke places the story, principally the lawyer's question, "Who is my neighbor?" It has been said that Jesus does not answer this question. At least not directly. Yet he does give answer in an existential way, by drawing us into a situation in which we intuit the answer. In fact, the story presents a classic answer to the ancient query of Cain, "Am I my brother's keeper?" (Gen. 4:9). Jesus' reply is profoundly primordial: "Every man in need is my neighbor, regardless of the risks involved." As for the nationality and status of the participants, they serve the same function as the characters of the other parables. The forgotten, the unlikely, and even the despised illuminate the presence of God's reign more than those we would naturally look to. Like the others, this parable is polemic. Established religion can be soporific, leading us into forgetfulness of God's redemptive presence, while the ordinary worldly acts of love, like this one, capture it elementally. We instinctively know what it means because we recognize the situation as our own, and are awakened out of forgetfulness into responsibility.

h. The crisis arising in Jesus' ministry of grace from the insensitivity of the "respectable righteous" is the theme of the parable of the great supper (Luke 14:15-24; Matthew's version, 22:1-14, is less original). The scene takes place in the house of a Pharisee (v. 1), and the parable itself is introduced by the pious utterance of someone at the table: "Blessed is he who shall eat bread in the kingdom of God." This remark is obviously offered by one who has not grasped the fact that the reign of God is already in action, that invitations have been sent out, that many are refusing to come, and others are being invited to fill their places. The parable proclaims a divine eschatology now in process of being realized. Jesus' reply is a rebuke of that kind of futurism implied by the words "shall eat." He says in effect: "The bread of the kingdom is here to be eaten now, and why are you refusing to eat it? That is why I have invited the unlikely from the streets and lanes of the city, the poor and maimed and blind and lame. It would be fine, you say, to be invited some future day to banquet in God's kingdom? Well, the kingdom is *here,* the banquet is going on, and you have turned it down!"

Parables of Process and Mystery

The upshot of the parabolic teaching so far is that the divine reign of grace has come, calling for men's decision to enter it. Jesus' emphasis on laying hold of this treasure means that it is a present possibility. Hence, the parables of process flow naturally from the others because their theme is basically the same. They also carry us into a third set of parables where future judgment and fruition of the kingdom are accented.

The remarkable point of the parables of growth, as Fuchs has noted, is the spirit of patience and waiting they engender.[8] Like the seed growing mysteriously, everything has its time (Eccles. 3:1). This is the heart of Jesus' teaching: he means to free his hearers from all anxiety about the future in order that they may concentrate upon the freedom of the present.

1. The parable of the seed growing mysteriously (Mark

4:26-29). This short piece reads well in the light of the parables already studied. Jesus consistently proclaims that the reign of God has broken into men's affairs in this new time. His focus is upon the present. We are then inclined to regard this parable as complete at the end of verse 28, taking verse 29 as an apocalyptic addition based on Joel 3:13: "Put in the sickle, for the harvest is ripe." The parable has been compared to the tares and the wheat (Matt. 13:24-30), but the likenesses are superficial. There the focus is on judgment and fulfillment, the end of the harvest. Here it is on the mysterious process of growth, not on the harvest itself. The seed grows by a mysterious power and is always creatively working, whether men sleep or go about their ordinary business. The creative power beyond man's control is illustrated by the man who scatters the seed, but "knows not how" the growth occurs; it happens *automatē,* "first the blade, then the ear, then the full grain in the ear." The kingdom of God is like that, Jesus says.

The parable does not at all suggest the modern view of inevitable progress, but rather the ultimate *mystery* of the creative process by which God works in the time of new planting. The seed has been sown and is growing quietly and irresistibly to harvest. We detect here a rebuke of those who might be thinking that the kingdom will be ushered in by a messianic revolt. No, not by an uprising, for the divine process of re-creation has unlikely beginnings and moves quietly but inexorably to remarkable fulfillment.

2. The parable of the sower (Mark 4:1-9). Perhaps the parable of the seed growing mysteriously sheds some light on this saying which has occasioned so many different interpretations. Is the parable of the sower not a joyful assurance that in spite of the loss of much seed and apparent failure, God has made a beginning that will yield a large harvest (v. 8)? In the realm of the kingdom, as in sowing, a bounteous harvest can be joyfully anticipated though some of the seed is

wasted, though some do not believe. It is a parable illustrating the irresistible process of divine creativity.

3. The parable of the mustard seed (Mark 4:30-32; cf. Luke 13:18 f.; Matt. 13:31 f., Q). Unremarkable beginnings, considerable endings: that is the theme of this third parable in the Markan series. The carpenter from Nazareth seems an unlikely medium for God's creative passage into the ways of men; his appearance is as unimpressive as a tiny grain of mustard seed. But the kingdom of God is a process of the unexpected. Jesus gives no clue as to the length of time involved in the growing process (a point worth remembering in considering Jesus' futurist teaching); his prime interest is that God is now at work. His understanding of time is thoroughly existentialist: the divine reign is in process in the concrete experience of the present.

We may also ask whether Jesus envisions the inclusion of the Gentiles, for the "birds of the air" which come and nest in the branches of the tree represent in apocalyptic and rabbinical literature the Gentile nations (cf. Dan. 4:12; Ezek. 17:22 f.; 31:6).

The parable suggests the divine reign which has come and moves creatively forward in every present moment toward fruition, spreading its branches along the way and sheltering the men of every station.

4. The parable of the leaven (Luke 13:20 f.; Matt. 13:33, Q). The contrast of littleness and largeness, of the small amount of leaven and the large mass of meal, gives us a clue to one possible meaning of this parable. Accent falls upon the dynamic process of God's reign in the world.

On the other hand, we recall that leaven is generally used in the Bible in a pejorative sense. It symbolizes the influence of evil. Could it be that Paul knew of this saying in its more original setting before Mark placed it among the parables of the kingdom? He warns the Corinthians that their boasting is bad, and that "a little leaven leavens the whole lump" (1

Cor. 5:6). He urges, "Cleanse out the old leaven that you may be a new lump, as you really are unleavened" (v. 7). It is questionable whether Jesus would make a positive identification of leaven and the process of the kingdom of God when the abhorrence of leaven was so strong in the Jewish tradition. Elsewhere Jesus speaks of "the leaven of the Pharisees and the leaven of Herod" (Mark 8:15; cf. Luke 12:1; Matt. 16:6). Is he perhaps warning his hearers that the kingdom is opposed by an insidious force of evil (Luke identifies it with hypocrisy) which can burst out of all proportion?

5. The parable of the wheat and the weeds (Matt. 13:24-30). If that is the case, then it stands close to the sense of this parable. The interpretation that Matthew gives it (13:36-43) is as full of detailed allegorizing as the interpretation of the parable of the sower in Mark, and we shall have to look beyond these churchly appropriations to the central thrust of the original parable.

If we strike out those verses that reflect editorial allegorizing (verses 25, 27, 28a), the parable becomes a simple illustration of a field of wheat mixed with weeds, a common enough sight in an agricultural setting. In the story, Jesus assumes that the kingdom has come and is growing like wheat in a field, hence the contrast between belief and unbelief. He is also warning of the danger of separating good and bad members in advance of God's judgment. The time for that has not yet come. Accordingly, Jesus refuses to form a separatist group like the Pharisees or Essenes, and so defends his invitation to publicans and sinners. Once more we have a polemic directed against those who criticize his ministry: "Let both grow together until the harvest."

Judgment in a final sense belongs to the future which stands in God's time. So does the full growth of wheat, the kingdom of God. The parable modulates into a third group which allows several clues to the future dimension of Jesus' eschatological teaching.

Parables of Warning, Judgment, and Fulfillment

This set of parables is integral to the others. Importantly, nearly every parable of Jesus implies a judgment, for in bringing the reign of God to every man, including the socially despised, he compels his people to take a stand. The scribes and Pharisees feel their authority threatened and resist, but in resisting God's new time of grace they judge their hypocrisy, for they have missed their mission as guardians of God's truth, and have shifted their guardianship to the precinct of legalism. Where divine love asserts itself, it not only blesses the receptive but judges the insensitive.

The parables in this group simply underscore the warning and judgment God's reign automatically brings; in several of them, Jesus looks to a future time of judgment and fulfillment, as already he has in the parable of the wheat and the weeds. As we might expect, these parables belong to the later phases of his ministry.

1. The parable of the wicked tenants (Mark 12:1-12; cf. Matt. 21:33-46; Luke 20:9-19). The heightening of the judgment motif finds a classic expression in this parable. It contains many allegorical touches and has been suspect for that reason, but there are good reasons for accepting it as substantially a genuine saying of Jesus (eliminating Mark 12:10 ff.). The setting is true to first-century Galilean life, for one thing. But since it is addressed to the chief priests, scribes, and elders in the temple (Mark 11:27, 12:12), it is designed to draw them into the story. Evidently it did: "They perceived that he had told the parable against them" (Mark 12:12). The thrust of the tale is a charge that the leaders of Israel have betrayed their trust and are to be called to account. Like the tenants of the vineyard, they have given shabby treatment to the prophets of God, and now they are ready to kill the owner's son. It is hard not to take this as Jesus' understanding of his mission, for the opposition to Jesus' ministry was such

at this point that he must have had a premonition of his passion. At any rate, the future holds a judgment for these men who have betrayed their responsibility to God by rejecting the messianic claims of Jesus.

2. The parable of the talents (Matt. 25:14-30; cf. Luke 19:12-27). When we put aside for the moment the application the early church gave this parable (understandable enough, for we do the same), it is clear that Jesus intended to compare the religionists with the third servant who failed to realize any return from the money entrusted to him. The official representatives of religion guarded the purity of their Judaism, but they faltered in their mission to the world. They buried a treasure in the ground; they must therefore render account to God.

3. The parable of the sheep and the goats (Matt. 25:31-46). One of the greatest of all the parables is this imaginary scene at the final assize of the world. Perhaps we should call it a visionary parable. Not all scholars accept its genuineness, but there is evidence to support its originality, especially the section dealing with the standards by which men are judged. We need not claim that every detail of the visionary parable is Jesus' own, yet the warmly human standard of judgment places it on the same footing as the other parables, and therefore begs our attention. It is in deeds of compassion toward the needy and despised that we are judged before God. And although the time of judgment is set in the future, the striking fact is that it is our action in the nonce which determines how we are to be judged. Indeed, we can say that every moment *is* the final assize, for we either grasp it or lose it in the face of our neighbor who is in need: "As you did it to one of the least of these my brethren, you did it to me" (Matt. 25:40).

Jesus' eschatology, then, is centrally existentialist. In the concrete situation where persons meet, the reign of God appears; there the new time is realized, and men seize it in love, or lose it in contempt. The kingdom of God is nowhere but here, in the creative processes of every moment, to be entered, to be seized, to be lived—or to be rejected.

Jesus may speak of a judgment to come, yet he asks us to live not for that moment but for the present where life is won or lost. For Jesus, every moment is full of redemptive possibility, charged with expectancy and impending crisis. The kingdom of God is like that. We are to be up to the moment, prepared, always.

4. This state of preparedness for seizing the moment is the central idea of three other parables which the early church, understandably enough, reapplied to the Lord's Second Coming, but which originally stood as exhortations to live for the immediate moment of the kingdom. Jesus bases the parables of the waiting servants (Luke 12:35-38), the thief at night (Luke 12:39; Matt. 24:43), and the ten maidens (Matt. 25: 1-13) upon ordinary, everyday experience in order to alert his hearers to the urgency of the kingdom. We are to live in electric excitement because every moment is crucial. Jesus never specifies the time of crisis and judgment which is to come because it is already in process of coming. We are to live every moment to the full because it is of ultimate significance.

5. That is the heart of Jesus' understanding of the kingdom of God, and it rests on his profound understanding of time. If the men of Israel can read the signs of weather in the sky, they ought to be able to see that the ministry of Jesus is the sign of God's time and that the reign of God has come upon them (Luke 12:54-56; Matt. 16:2-3, Q). But the scribes and Pharisees are blind to the time, their eye is unsound and their light turned to darkness (Matt. 6:22 f.; Luke 11:34-36, Q). They do not realize the hypocrisy of their position. Thinking themselves secure, they have no more security than the rich fool who dreamed of larger barns and years of ease and prosperity, but who was called to account that very night (Luke 12:16-20).

6. If a man claims to be something but fails to back up his word, he is compared to salt that has lost its savor and is thrown out (Luke 14:34 f.; Matt. 5:13, Q). This metaphor illustrates in the simplest way that an authentic person is one whose speech, behavior, and intention are integral. The time of the kingdom calls for personal wholeness.

7. If we underestimate the importance of authentic living, assuming that we can be faithless for the moment on the chance that there is plenty of time later to become serious about life, we are compared to the servant vested with authority (Luke 12:42-46; Matt. 24:45-51, Q). He is unhappily surprised when the master comes back unexpectedly. The church applied it to faithful living before Christ's return in glory (as we reapply it existentially to our own setting), but originally Jesus directed it to the leaders of religion who had failed to keep their trust. It is a parable of exhortation and judgment.

8. This carries us to the last in our analysis, the parable of the unmerciful servant (Matt. 18:23-35). This seems at first glance a negative saying, but in reality it presents us with the existential choice of the hour. The forgiveness of the kingdom is what we have already received, just as the servant is forgiven his debt by his lord. Are we or are we not, then, to forgive others? The responsibility of the sons of the kingdom is *to become* what they have *received,* otherwise they reveal their hypocrisy and judge themselves.

Wholeness or hypocrisy, compassion or contempt—these are the existential themes running through the parables. The time of the kingdom of God has come, is coming, and will continue to come as the "field" of men's existence. Central to the attention Jesus gives to the dimensions of time—that it has come or is yet to come—is the tremendous importance of the present and the need for personal wholeness in every moment. It is this existential understanding of time and of personal integrity that marks the parabolic language of Jesus and gives it its timely relevance. It also provides us with clues to an understanding of the person of Jesus himself.

The parables of Jesus are so primordial, concrete, existential, and personal that they deserve pride of place in this study of the kingdom. They have already provided us with Jesus' fundamental understanding of existence and witnessed to his self-understanding and mission. They also serve as a check against a tendency of the early church to speculate rather too much on the apocalyptic details of the future. We will have to come back again and again to the parables, for they stand at the heart of Jesus' proclamation of the kingdom.

READINGS ON CHAPTER TWO

Beare, Frank W. *The Earliest Records of Jesus.* New York: Abingdon Press, 1962. A companion to *Gospel Parallels: A Synopsis of the First Three Gospels.* New York: Thomas Nelson & Sons, 1949. (Greek edition by Huck-Lietzmann-Cross. Oxford: Basil Blackwell, 1954.)

Dodd, C. H. *The Parables of the Kingdom.* London: Nisbet & Co., 1953.

Fuchs, Ernst. *Studies of the Historical Jesus.* Translated by Andrew Scobie. ("Studies in Biblical Theology," No. 42.) London: SCM Press, 1964.

Funk, Robert W. *Language, Hermeneutic, and Word of God.* New York: Harper & Row, 1966.

Grant, Robert M. *A Historical Introduction to the New Testament.* New York: Harper & Row, 1963.

Hunter, A. M. *Interpreting the Parables.* Philadelphia: Westminster Press, 1960.

Jeremias, Joachim. *The Parables of Jesus.* Translated by S. H. Hooke. London: SCM Press, 1963.

Manson, T. W. *The Teaching of Jesus.* Cambridge: Cambridge University Press, 1955.

Robinson, James M., and Cobb, John B., Jr. (eds.). *New Frontiers in Theology.* Vol. II: *The New Hermeneutic.* New York: Harper & Row, 1964.

Sewell, Elizabeth. *The Human Metaphor*. South Bend, Ind.: University of Notre Dame Press, 1964.

Thielicke, Helmut. *The Waiting Father*. Translated by John W. Doberstein. New York: Harper & Row, 1959.

Wilder, Amos N. *The Language of the Gospel: Early Christian Rhetoric*. New York: Harper & Row, 1964.

CHAPTER THREE

The
Eschatological Sayings
of the
Kingdom

AN EXAMINATION of the parables has provided an entry into a closer study of the ministry of Jesus. This beginning places a strong emphasis on the concrete historical setting of Jesus' ministry. The modern tendency of some New Testament interpreters to concentrate overmuch upon the Word has led to a de-emphasis of the situations in which Jesus proclaimed his message. Words have a setting, always, and any attempt to abstract them from their concreteness does less than full justice to an important dimension of personal existence.

The sayings of Jesus that we turn to now can easily be abstracted from their situations and misformed by isolated linguistic or theological inquiries. But this study is based on an acceptance of the parables as the hermeneutical norm, which means that the other sayings of Jesus will be entered into by way of his situational, or existential, understanding of the new time of the kingdom.

This chapter deals with those eschatological sayings of Jesus judged to be his own, which reveal further dimensions of his understanding of time and the kingdom. The chapter following will consider the enigmatic Son of man sayings and Jesus' use of the term in light of his other language.

It is not necessary to assume the detailed historicity of the Marcan order of Jesus' ministry which Matthew and Luke follow in their generally similar accounts, for all three Synoptists are shaping the historical material according to their individual style and perception of Jesus. The early witnesses to Jesus' ministry show considerable creativity in the various combinations and arrangements they employ to present their portraits of Jesus.

The variety of witnesses and combinations of materials evidence a fundamental fact about knowing, which can be called *complementary aspection.* The aspects of a person we get to know are complemented by what others discover when they participate in that same life.

All we need know about the order of Jesus' ministry is that at some point he began to preach and heal, and at last underwent a final passion and was crucified. What transpires in between need not and cannot be placed in any exact order of progression. What we do find in the Gospels are nodal situations or episodes, similar to the parables, which engage us existentially. It does not actually matter too much that a precise sequence of events is beyond our ken. We can be satisfied with episodes from a personal life. In this respect, the parables are instructive because they present us with self-contained situations, nodular episodes, each of which has the power to involve us personally and awaken us out of forgetfulness.

Proclamation of the Kingdom

1. The Sermon on the Mount has this episodal dynamic, in spite of its being a composite arrangement by the author of the First Gospel. In these sayings of Jesus, which are at once in the great tradition of the wisdom sayings of the Old Testament, yet eschatological to the core, Jesus reiterates the tremendous theme of the unity of motive and action. It is gestalt preaching at its profoundest level. Acts are not what a man hides behind (Marcel calls these mere gestures),[1] but what he

stands behind with personal integrity. This is the wholeness the kingdom of God brings, and with its coming the hypocrisy of legalistic casuistry is exposed for what it is.

To understand the sermon we must see it in the light of Jesus' proclamation of the kingdom. The kingdom brings us a new relationship with God and with our neighbor. The standards of the sermon are not universal maxims which Jesus espouses for all to admire, but expressions of gratitude for the gift of grace the kingdom brings. Jeremias has written splendidly of this in his study, *The Sermon on the Mount,* where he presents a convincing case for viewing the so-called sermon in its present form as a catechism of instruction in the early Christian church.[2] The Sermon on the Mount assumes that the gift of new life has been received because the time of salvation is present. This teaching is not law, and it does not belong to the context of the Old Testament and Judaism. It is rather an expression of grace which is being experienced because the kingdom has come.

This is true of the individual sayings of Jesus which make up the composite Sermon on the Mount. These utterances were originally spoken on various occasions. Each saying is a summary of a sermon by Jesus, comprising proclamation and instruction *(kerygma and didachē).* The theme, as in the parables, consistently emphasizes the integral unity of word and deed. In fact, Matthew combines into a unit the didactic teaching of chapters 5-7 with a collection of miracle stories in chapters 8-9 to show the inseparable presence of language and act in Jesus the Messiah, who eminently manifests the new era of wholeness. His theme is Jesus' own, encapsulated in the great saying, "Unless your righteousness exceeds that of the scribes and Pharisees, you will never enter the kingdom of heaven" (Matt. 5:20). The reign of God signifies wholeness, and whenever that is proclaimed in word or deed, it comes into conflict with hypocrisy, where motives, words, and acts are sundered. And that is the identical motif of the parables.

Three kinds of righteousness are contrasted in this saying. The scribes were the professional theologians; and the Pharisees, pious laymen of many professions of whom only a few were theologians. We should be careful not to criticize them as a group (the fallacy of the part equals the whole), for there were doubtless many who evinced a genuine piety. But Jesus had enough experience with some of them to know that their intricate legalism tended toward hollow casuistry. He contrasts the righteousness of the kingdom, which is fidelity, to the righteousness of legalism, which is gesture.

The Sermon on the Mount as it stands in Matthew is a catechism for Jewish-Christian converts who have already experienced newness of life (the differences in Luke's arrangement indicate a Gentile-Christian setting). But incorporated within it are sayings of Jesus which assume an identical prerequisite: the renewal of one's life by the grace of the kingdom precedes instruction for action.

Let us look at several of these original sayings, or logia, of Jesus which bear out the presence of the kingdom in his ministry, keeping in mind the leitmotiv of Matthew 5:20 which equates the kingdom with a righteousness of wholeness. Use will be made of Jeremias' five examples:[3]

a. "You are the light of the world" (Matt. 5:14). To compare the disciples with the sun assumes that the disciples have found the light of the world in Jesus (John 8:12).

b. The saying of Matthew 6:15, "If you do not forgive men their trespasses, neither will your Father forgive your trespasses," is really the same as the conclusion to the parable of the unmerciful servant (Matt. 18:35), in which the call to forgive and the warning of judgment is preceded by forgiveness. Being forgiven requires that one forgive. If he refuses, he hears the words of judgment: "So also my heavenly Father will do to every one of you, if you do not forgive your brother from your heart."

c. The third example is the saying on divorce (Matt. 5:31-32) which seems to be a harsh criticism of the Torah (Deut. 24:1). The point is that Jesus' opponents rely on the Law, while Jesus goes back to the paradisal will of God in the creation story. Jesus is saying that the primordial will of God is expressing itself again in this new time of renewal.

d. Matthew 5:44-45 is the command to love our enemies, presupposing the presence of the unbounded goodness of God.

e. Finally, the admonition to turn the other cheek (Matt. 5:38-39) is not a maxim about insults in general but a specific instruction on how the disciples should take the charge of heresy. Every word of Jesus about calumny, persecution, and dishonor to the disciples assumes that they stand in the prophetic tradition (Isa. 50:6), and therefore will gladly accept their prior calling and responsibility to proclaim the kingdom of God.

"Something preceded," Jeremias remarks,[4] and that something is the presence of the reign of God proclaimed by Jesus. The new age has come.

Jesus also contrasts the old era with the new in the remarkable words, "You have heard that it was said . . . , but I say to you." His authority is unmistakable as he assumes the prerogative of a new Moses and proclaims the new Torah of fidelity. The new time is personified in the personal pronoun "I," referring to Jesus himself. It is the integrity of his word, deed, and intention which speaks with new authority.

If Jesus announces the reconciling reign of God in the supreme moment of the now, he enjoins his disciples to manifest their fidelity in the present moment also. They are to become the salt of the earth (Matt. 5:13), the light of the world (Matt. 5:14), following the way of love (Matt. 5:43-48). Here, in the *fidelity* of love which the kingdom brings, love of God and love of man become one, so that in the profoundest sense our love of neighbor is the test of our love of God.

Jesus accords extreme importance to personal fidelity as a mark of the kingdom. The point is brought out in Matthew 5:20, treated previously. But the Sermon on the Mount repeats the theme again and again, as though Jesus' single role were to impress his disciples with the truth that the difference between the way of God and the way of the demonic is the difference between healing and hating, wholeness and hypocrisy. Each of the "But I say to you" sayings thrusts directly to personal motives, contrasting external display to internal integrity.

These are remarkable sayings, not only because of their content, but for their use of "I." That Jesus would contrast himself with Moses was unheard of for a rabbi. These scholars might use the phrase in debate with one another, but never to set themselves above Moses. In these antitheses (of which the first, second, and fourth are beyond any doubt authentic) Jesus claims a messianic authority far above the rabbinical and prophetic traditions.

It is then the unitary self, the gestalt, that lies central to all his words. Elsewhere, the contrast is drawn between God and Legion, where the unwhole man has lost his unity and become many (Mark 5:9; Luke 8:30). The splitting of motives from words and words from works is like demonic possession because it destroys a man and renders the relation of persons impossible.

In the Sermon on the Mount this contrast is made again in the warning not to sound a trumpet when giving alms, as the playactors do (Matt. 6:2-4), nor to heap up empty phrases when praying (Matt. 6:5-8), nor to look dismal when fasting, as though this were a great sign of piety (Matt. 6:16-18). Instead, the disciple is to evince a singleness of purpose (Matt. 6:24) and a sound eye (Matt. 6:22-23) which first removes the log from its own vision before it criticizes the speck in another's (Matt. 7:1-5). The kingdom makes a double impression: first, it announces the eschatological time of renewal and reaffirms the paradisal themes of wholeness, for those who love with the love of the kingdom hold no brief for divorce or hate; second, the announcement of the presence of grace creates a tension between what we are and what we should become. Eschatology is inseparable from ethics. Good news requires self-examination, then decision, followed by responsible fidelity.

The metaphor of the two trees (Matt. 7:16-17) and the parable of the two houses (Matt. 7:24-27) round off the Matthean arrangement with sayings of self-examination. If the Socratic dictum that the unexamined life is not worth living is given an existential turn, it could not be more appropriate to this tale, whose only purpose is to make the hearer examine the foundations of his life. And this is a theme that is central to the whole sermon.

Two other sections of the Sermon on the Mount must be mentioned. The first is the Lord's Prayer (Matt. 6:9-13). Reference has already been made to the tension that arises from the kingdom's presence and the ethics of the kingdom. We feel this tension, as the disciples certainly did, between the possibilities of the new time and our failure to lay hold of these possibilities completely. But the tension is not only a mark of our experience, it belongs to the nature of the kingdom itself. It has come, it comes, and it is yet to come. The Lord's Prayer expresses this tension in devotional utterances of remarkable character. First it presents our praise of God whose name is holy over all. Our worship is focused in vertical dimension toward the ultimate of all our concerns. Then the vertical flows into the lateral when we pray,

> Thy kingdom come,
> Thy will be done,
> On earth as it is in heaven.

The lateral dimension of history is the area of God's creativity, and we pray for the continual coming of his reign in the concrete episodes of our experience. A tension is set up between the now and the not yet. The prayer is a magnificent expression of eschatology in process. It expresses thanks for the kingdom wherein we are fed, forgiven, and delivered. It then asks that God's reign will continue to come, and overcome, that the heavenly kingdom (God's primordial, paradisal will for man) may be realized on earth. It is a prayer of praise, thanksgiving, confession, and expectation.

Jesus is silent on the question of when and how the consummation of the kingdom is to take place. His only concern is to say, in effect, that since the reign of grace is here and the future belongs to God, we may confidently expect the grace of the kingdom to be present in every future moment as it passes into our present. We are freed from anxiety of an unknown and meaningless future (Matt. 6:25-34), freed to live joyfully, confidently, and creatively in the present. It is to the present that Jesus frees us, to ourselves and to one another where we are, in the very presence of God's own creativity.

A final word needs to be said about the Beatitudes, especially the first and third: "Blessed are the poor in spirit, for theirs is the kingdom of heaven" (Matt. 5:3; cf. Luke 6:20); and "Blessed are the meek, for they shall inherit the earth" (Matt. 5:5). These sayings are as thoroughly eschatological as the other utterances of Jesus. They set up a dramatic relationship between the present and future dimensions of the kingdom. The presence of God's reign is proclaimed in the words "Blessed are" and "theirs is," and its future coming is established in the promise "they shall." The meek, the humble, the poor, are witnesses to the reversal of values that the kingdom brings in the now and will bring in the time yet to come.

A remarkable parallel to this comes out of 4QpPs 37 1:8 f. of the Qumran texts, in which the members of the community call themselves "the Poor" and anticipate the eschatological hope of God:

And the humble shall inherit the earth and they shall delight in the abundance of peace. The interpretation of this concerns [the congregation of the] Poor who accept the time of affliction; they will be delivered from all the snares.[5]

Here we have a commentary on Psalm 37:11: "But the meek shall possess the land, and delight themselves in abundant prosperity," which is an ancient eschatological hope of reversal echoed again in Matthew 23:12: "Whoever exalts himself will be humbled, and whoever humbles himself will be exalted" (cf. Matt. 18:4; Luke 14:11; 18:14); and "Many that are first will be last, and the last first" (Mark 10:31). This is eschatology in process of realization.

2. The leitmotiv of continually realized eschatology, or process eschatology, is beautifully expressed in Mark's summary of Jesus' proclamation of the gospel (Mark 1:15). Here are the three elements of kerygmatic preaching: first, the announcement that the messianic time (*kairos*) is fulfilled and the new age inaugurated; second, that the kingdom of God "has come upon" the world (*ēggiken*); and third, that the hearer is to repent and believe. Now, as we shall see in Part II of this study, the early church uses exactly the same outline in its kerygma.

The first and third points are almost identical: the expression the "fullness of time" is reminiscent of Galatians 4:4; Ephesians 1:9-10; Acts 2:16-21; 3:18; and the imperative "repent" of Acts 2:38; 3:19. In the second part, the metaphor of the kingdom of God which figures so prominently in Jesus' teaching is virtually dropped in favor of Jesus himself, whom the church comes to recognize as the personification of the kingdom. Jesus the Christ becomes the kingdom for the early church.

The eschatological saying of Mark 1:15 may reflect Mark's summary touch, but there is no doubt that it accurately sums up the points of Jesus' proclamation. In his words and acts he proclaims the arrival of the new time, he preaches the presence of the kingdom of God, he calls for repentance. But what is especially of interest here is the meaning of the word *ēggiken*. It is important because it stands in a saying at the beginning of Jesus' ministry. On the one hand, it cannot mean "has come" in the fullest sense of the term. (C. H. Dodd may be excused for overplaying realized eschatology at this point; he was trying to make a case and he made it too well.) On the other hand, we shall have to close our eyes to every evidence of the kingdom in Jesus' ministry in order to give the verb *ēggiken* a completely futurist meaning as Schweitzer and Bultmann have elected to do. Schweitzer was unable to carry his case in the court of scholars, and Bultmann is finding it increasingly difficult to uphold his own.

The long controversy encircling this word has, in my opinion, suggested a quite satisfactory answer. It generally means "has drawn near," but it also carries the sense of coming up to or arriving. In Acts 21:33, for example, "the tribune came up (*ēggisas*) and arrested [Paul]," which suggests something more than drawing near. Again, Luke 24:28 reads, "By this time they had reached (*ēggisan*) the village to which they were going, and he made as if to continue his journey," as *The New English Bible* correctly renders it.[6]

It is also best to translate Matthew 26:45 "The hour has come" (*ēggiken hē hōra*). Matthew is probably using Mark 14:41 as his source, and Mark interestingly employs the stronger verb *ēlthen* to render the same saying. It has been suggested that Matthew is purposely trying to correct Mark to show that the hour was not Jesus' arrest but his death. But it is much more likely that the "hour" comprises the whole series of events from the arrest to the crucifixion, that at the arrest the hour of the final passion has begun, and that Matthew and Mark understood it in this sense. (It is worthwhile noting that the Fourth Gospel also uses the word hour in the sense of arrival as well as expectancy: "But the hour is coming, and now is," John 4:23). Moreover, in the accounts of

Matthew 26:46-47 and Mark 14:42-43, while Jesus is still speaking the words, "my betrayer is upon us (*ēggiken*)," "Judas came (*ēlthen*)." This allows for the interpretation that the former verb lends itself to a certain flexibility.

The verb *eggizō* may therefore imply nearness, but it may also suggest arrival. The kingdom of God participates in the tension of the now and the not yet.

The reign of God has already begun to exert itself in Jesus' ministry, in view of the remarkable saying of Luke 11:20 and Matthew 12:28, Q: "But if it is by the finger [Spirit] of God that I cast out demons, then the kingdom of God has come upon you (*ephthasen*)."[7] Here the sense of arrival is unmistakable but it is also associated with an invasion of demonic evil which is open-ended, for Jesus continues his warfare against the demonic to his very death, and it continues into the present. The tension remains: the kingdom has come, but not completely come, which is the elemental theme of the parables. Eschatology is always in process of being realized and hence partakes of the multidimensionality, the tension, and the mystery of personal existence.

3. This interpretation of eschatology squares well with the pericope of Mark 2:23-28 about the plucking of ears of corn on the sabbath, except that this episode reveals the tension between the was and now is, between the old law and the new, and introduces us to a new term, the Son of man. Here is another one of those truly remarkable utterances of fidelity versus gesture which is so characteristic of Jesus' message. The Pharisees accuse him of breaking the sabbath law, which denies a man the right to satisfy his hunger by taking a handful of grain from someone's field of corn. This activity is allowed on any other day of the week, but not on the workless sabbath. Plucking grain is harvesting, and rubbing it out to eat is threshing. It is difficult to imagine a legalism weightier than that.

Now the question is, Which of the final sayings in the

pericope is more original? Is it verse 28, "So the Son of man is lord even of the sabbath," or verse 27, "The sabbath was made for man, not man for the sabbath"? The Aramaic underlying both "Son of man" and "man" would have been *barnasha* (correctly "son of man"), but then it is hard to understand why the same phrase should be translated two ways. It has been suggested that in both cases it meant either "man" or "Son of man," but since it would have been unlikely for Jesus to say that "Man is Lord of the sabbath" the preferred reading should be, "The sabbath was made for the Son of man, not the Son of man for the sabbath" (v. 27).[8]

It is difficult to settle this question because of the enigmatic character of the Son of man sayings. For example, Heinz Tödt, in his recent study, *The Son of Man in the Synoptic Tradition* (1959, Eng. trans. 1965), considers all the sayings in detail and concludes that the genuine Son of man utterances are Matthew 24:27 and para.; 24:37, 39 and para.; 24:44; Mark 8:38 and para.; Luke 11:30; 12:8 f. and para.; 17:30. Mark 2:28 is not one of them. He believes the early church has raised the saying of verse 27 into an utterance of lordship in which Jesus personally claims authority over the sabbath.[9]

Now we could argue against Tödt that the "But I say to you" antitheses in the Sermon on the Mount are clear assertions of Jesus that he claims a higher authority than the Torah, and that Mark 2:27 is one further instance of that authority. We could also remark that Tödt's use of the critical method is rather more severe than it needs to be, and attaches too much creativity to the community and too little originality to Jesus. This last is important in deciding whether a saying is Jesus' own or a Christian comment.

Yet there is a sense in which the simple reading "man" in Mark 2:27 has an existential significance of singular importance. Though it may not be the original reading, it declares a freedom from the past which for Jesus is a keynote of the new time. Jesus embodies the new Torah ("The Son of man is lord of the sabbath") and in his declaration of authority reestablishes the paradisal freedom of man. He embodies the freedom which liberates man from the burdensome weight and gesture of ceremony. The Son of man is a corporate term with its roots in the apocalyptic Book of Daniel. There the figure of the Son of man (Dan. 7:13 f.), to whom the Ancient of Days gives dominion and glory and kingdom, is identified with the saints of the Most High, who shall receive the kingdom and possess it forever (Dan. 7:18).

If Jesus uses the term Son of man in the sense of this passage in Daniel, he carries on the great Jewish tradition of personally embodying his people, even as the patriarchs Abraham, Isaac, and Jacob, and the lawgiver Moses sum up the whole of Israel in the particularity of their persons. The Son of man is accordingly a corporate term—one might even say a punctiliar term—which expresses the unity of Jesus and man. Certainly the early church thought corporately of the unity of Christ and his people, and undoubtedly they discovered the corporate theme in Jesus.

Now if this is the case, then it is precisely because Jesus is the lord of the sabbath, the new Moses so to speak, that he is also the Son of man who speaks in behalf of every man. In him an elemental truth is rescued from forgetfulness: "The sabbath was made for man, not man for the sabbath." That is the declaration of freedom Jesus makes in his personal words and acts.

It appears that the topics of the kingdom of God and the Son of man deal with the same existential themes and find their unity in the person of Jesus. They are in fact practically identical.

We shall look at the other Son of man sayings later. For now, however, the remaining kingdom sayings in the Synoptics need to be examined with an eye to the criteria laid down in this study of the parables.

The Coming of the Kingdom

1. Mark 9:1 (Matt. 14:28; Luke 9:27) is not an easy saying to interpret. *The New English Bible* translates it, "There are some of those standing here who will not taste death before they have seen the kingdom of God already come in power." This seems to reveal the hand of C. H. Dodd, the general editor of *The New English Bible*. He had argued earlier in *The Parables of the Kingdom* that Jesus is predicting that his hearers will soon come to see with their understanding (not simply with their eyes) that the kingdom has been powerfully in their midst all the while, though at the present time they are unable to divine its working. This is certainly an ingenious and plausible interpretation, because the parabolic message of Jesus leaves no doubt that he proclaims the present activity of God's reign.

The only drawback is that the verb *horan* (to see) has to be strained to carry the sense of seeing with intellectual perception. We are better off to stay with the usual translation, which seems more natural: "There are some standing here who will not taste death before they see the kingdom of God come with power." Jesus does not mean, then, that some will come to realize before very long that the kingdom has *already* come with power, where before they failed to realize it, but that some of them will see with their own eyes (not just intellectually) a new and powerful manifestation of the kingdom. The saying refers to the future.

Does Jesus expect the future coming of the kingdom "in power" (*en dynamei*) to be a world-shattering visitation of God in the sense of radical apocalyptic thought? Possibly, but the words "in power" may give us a clue to the sense of the saying. Paul uses the same expression in Romans 1:4 when he proclaims that Jesus was "designated Son of God *in power* according to the Spirit of holiness by his resurrection from the dead."* Could Jesus have anticipated a future outpouring of the grace of the kingdom in the kind of power released in the resurrection? This is conjectural, and perhaps it is better simply to say that the utterance in Mark 9:1 reveals the tension in Jesus' teaching between the kingdom already in action and its coming in fuller dimension in future. To read too much into Jesus' understanding of the details of the future is risky; it is preferable simply to make the point that for him the hidden working of the kingdom in the present is going to be manifested dynamically in the future. Because this theme is common to the parables, it is better to assume that the saying is Jesus' own (against Bultmann and his school) and that this expression of tension between present and future gave rise to the early church's own tension regarding the present working of the Holy Spirit and the Second Coming of Christ. In Jesus' expectation, the future is described as the eschatological messianic banquet, the new temple, the "day" or "coming" of the Son of man, or as here, the coming of the kingdom of God in power.

The principal point is that the future belongs to God, releasing us from anxiety that we may be free in the present where God's activity is already at work. It is impossible to say with certainty whether Jesus was in error about the time of the future manifestation or foresaw the fruition of his ministry in the momentous event surrounding his death. But perhaps the fact that the catena of sayings in Mark 8:34—9:1 links the sufferings of Jesus' disciples with his own should serve to remind us that for Mark (who is writing during the time of the Neronian persecution), Christians can take hope: Jesus lost his life and found it—so may they. Suffering will be followed by resurrection. And because the future belongs to them, so does the present. The whole passage has the tone

---

*Italics added here and in subsequent Scripture quotations.

of joyful expectation, if one is first willing to take up his cross and follow Jesus.

2. Mark 14:25 (Matt. 26:29; cf. Luke 22:16, 18) uses the biblical symbolism of Isaiah 25:6-8 to depict the future banquet at which all the people of God will eat and drink together. The marriage feast has already begun in Jesus' ministry (Mark 2:19), but the messianic banquet has its future dimension: "I tell you, many will come from east and west and sit at table with Abraham, Isaac, and Jacob in the kingdom of heaven" (Matt. 8:11). This looks forward to the future activity of God, which Jesus anticipates in the present verse (Mark 14:25) when he says at the institution of the Last Supper: "Truly, I say to you, I shall not drink again of the fruit of vine until that day when I drink it new in the kingdom of God." The Lord's Supper symbolizes the messianic banquet that has already begun in his ministry and that anticipates fulfillment. The dimensions of time symbolized by the feast are nicely encapsulated in the eucharistic words of Paul: "For as often as you eat this bread and drink the cup, you proclaim the Lord's death until he comes" (1 Cor. 11:26). The same tension between past, present, and future in Jesus' teaching of the kingdom is transposed to the church's own experience. It remembers, it anticipates, it is set free in the present and rejoices. It is freed from the legalism of the past, freed from anxiety of the future, freed for creative fidelity in the present.

3. How then does the kingdom come? The answer is couched in the mysterious words: "The kingdom of God is not coming with signs to be observed; nor will they say, 'Lo, here it is!' or 'There!' for behold, the kingdom of God is in the midst of you" (Luke 17:20b-21). Here is a truly remarkable saying. There is little doubt that in this context the Greek preposition *entos* means "in your midst" and not "within you," which would not fit at all with Jesus' teaching elsewhere that the kingdom is primarily God's activity in history, not initially

an inner disposition of the psyche. The great importance of the saying is to be found in its interpretation of history. Jesus rejects all sign-calculation of the kingdom's coming (cf. the similar warning in the short apocalypse of Mark 13:21; Matt. 24:23). Reading the signs of God's supposed predetermined plan was an elaborate concern in apocalyptic thought (e.g., Dan. 10:21; 1 Enoch 103:2).

But Jesus refuses to speak in these terms. The kingdom of God is a dynamic process which is sudden and unexpected, requiring the readiness of men to respond to its coming. The kingdom is always coming in unexpected ways, and will continue to come unexpectedly in the future. Jesus is much closer, then, to the Old Testament prophets with their profound understanding of the importance of the moment than he is to the apocalyptic seers.

There is also a possibility that Jesus is making a veiled reference to himself when he says that "the kingdom of God is in the midst of you." In the antitheses of the Sermon on the Mount, he assumes the remarkable authority of a new Moses. He claims that in his invasion of the demonic realm the kingdom of God has come (Matt. 12:28; Luke 11:20, Q), and much of his language has a particularity about it which refers us to his person. Is he saying that he embodies the reign of God and makes it present by being in their midst? That is very likely. Such an idea would certainly be opposed to all the usual "signs" of apocalyptic calculation. The very idea that a man could personally embody the kingship of God would be highly unusual and unexpected. We know all too well that Jesus' announcement that the kingdom was coming in his ministry invited violent opposition.

4. Violence is the theme of the difficult saying of Matthew 11:12: "From the days of John the Baptist until now the kingdom of heaven has suffered violence (*biazetai*), and men of violence (*biastai*) take it by force (*harpazousin*)." It has

77

been suggested by a number of interpreters that the verb *biazetai* should be translated as a middle rather than as a passive to allow the reading, "The kingdom of heaven exercises its power, and men of violence snatch at it." The "men of violence" would then be those willing to take every risk to enter it. That would seem to accord with the parallel reading of Luke 16:16: "The law and the prophets were until John; since then the good news of the kingdom of God is preached, and every one enters it violently."

But it is likelier that the first reading is more original because in fact the kingdom does suffer violence from its enemies while it is invading the demonic realm. In the holy war writings of the Qumran sect the Sons of Light will suffer setbacks from the Sons of Darkness before they are victorious (IQM 1:12; cf. IQH). And the day of Israel's restoration in Jeremiah 30:7 is full of distress until Jacob is finally saved out of it. There are precedents, then, for viewing the activity of the kingdom as a serious conflict in which losses are incurred in the war against evil. Since the saying occurs in the context of John the Baptist's imprisonment (Matt. 11:2-19) and imminent death, it is likely that Jesus sees the beginning of the new era of the kingdom in the days of John the Baptist, and evidence of its working in the acts of violence committed against it.

In any event, whether Matthew 11:12 is a saying about the violence done to the kingdom or of the kingdom exercising its own power, the point is hard to miss that the reign of God is at work in the ministry of Jesus. If the Revised Standard Version reading is correct, the kingdom of God undergoes personal attack in the Baptist's imprisonment and death. By implication Jesus is also under attack by common opponents. The kingdom is identified with the ministries of John the Baptist and Jesus. The difference between the two is that while John introduces the shift of the eras, his message is ascetic and judgmental, and only initiates the kingship of God.

78

Jesus, however, develops this first period of the kingdom and opens up its potentials for grace and healing. That is why Jesus can speak of the kingdom as suffering violence since the days of John the Baptist (Matt. 11:12) and yet affirm in the same breath that great as the Baptist is, his ministry does not represent the fullness of grace which the least of Jesus' disciples have already experienced (Matt. 11:11). John introduces and Jesus personally embodies the kingdom, yet both suffer the violent calumny of their common critics, who are likened to children at sport in the marketplace, condemning the Baptist for asceticism and Jesus for frequenting with sinners.

5. The fact that the Baptist is the initiator but not the full bearer of the kingdom accounts for Jesus' reply to his query, recorded in Matthew 11:3, "Are you he who is to come, or shall we look for another?" John realizes that he has played only a preparatory role in the coming of the new era, but he is not sure whether Jesus is really the bearer of the good tidings of the kingdom. Jesus' response is a striking affirmation of the presence of divine kingship in his words and deeds. He instructs his disciples to tell John what they have personally heard and seen: "The blind receive their sight and the lame walk, lepers are cleansed and the deaf hear, and the dead are raised up, and the poor have good news preached to them" (Matt. 11:5).

6. Hearing and seeing the signs of the kingdom in Jesus' teaching and healing accounts for the blessedness of the disciples: "Blessed are the eyes which see what you see! For I tell you that many prophets and kings desired to see what you see, and did not see it, and to hear what you hear, and did not hear it" (Luke 10:23-24). It is important to compare this saying with Matthew 11:3, 11 in order to understand why Jesus claimed John the Baptist as a harbinger of the kingdom and yet distinguished his own ministry radically from John's. In Jesus the kingship of God is literally em-

bodied in word and act. John announces the kingdom—Jesus personifies the kingdom.

7. Another "sign" saying which attests the presence of the new time of the kingdom is Luke 11:31 f.; Matthew 12:41 f., Q:

The queen of the South will arise at the judgment with the men of this generation and condemn them; for she came from the ends of the earth to hear the wisdom of Solomon, and behold, something greater than Solomon is here. The men of Nineveh will arise at the judgment with this generation and condemn it; for they repented at the preaching of Jonah, and behold, something greater than Jonah is here.

This extraordinary saying begs careful analysis. It affirms that "something greater than Solomon" and "something greater than Jonah *is here*." The "something greater" is a neuter adjective and may very well be a periphrasis for the kingdom of God or Jesus himself, or both. The teaching is unmistakable: something surpassing two great nodular figures in Israel's tradition has come. It is likely that Jesus is using this indirect manner of speaking to contrast with himself two historic Hebrew figures, one a man of wisdom and the other a prophet.

The Matthean version bears the marks of Christian interpretation (Matt. 12:40). In using the story of Jonah's three days and three nights in the belly of the whale as a symbol of the Son of man's burial in the heart of the earth, Matthew is introducing the church's resurrection theology. This is surely secondary. Luke stays closer to the original saying. He understands correctly that the sign of Jonah is an allusion to the simple preaching of repentance, devoid of any other signs than the word of Yahweh. The Ninevites respond to Jonah's word without further proof, as the queen of Sheba gratefully receives the wisdom of Solomon (1 Kings 10:1-13). Together they will testify against a generation, Jesus' own, which is unreceptive to the grace of the kingdom.

These ancient witnesses "will arise at the judgment," because the kingdom is future as well as present. So the dimensions of divine kingship are not only temporal but ethical, for the reign of God brings judgment as well as grace. This saying is unusually instructive. It concerns, first, the question of time: the past is superseded by the present and the present moves on to a future which is God's. It concerns, second, the existential question of decision: the present is full of possibility for belief or unbelief, reconciliation or refusal, good or bad, love or hate, redemption or judgment.

Entering the Kingdom

Finally, after noting again the importance of personal responsibility, which is the central theme of Jesus' message, we need to look at a last group of kingdom sayings having to do with receiving and entering the kingdom.

It is not really important whether the Marcan outline of the ministry is accurate in detail, since the parables and kingdom sayings provide us with an impressive body of teaching that enables us to meet the historical Jesus on a very elemental, personal level. The parables allow us a most direct access into his intentionality, and of course they do not depend upon any detailed sequence of events in his ministry.

All the same, it is rather striking that Mark, together with Matthew and Luke who follow the Marcan framework, arrange the kingdom sayings in a theological sequence. When the sayings are listed in their order of appearance, a distinct change of emphasis takes place in chapter nine of Mark, following Peter's confession of Jesus' messiahship at Caesarea Philippi (Mark 8:27-33). Before the confession Jesus proclaims the coming of the kingdom, and afterward he urges men to enter it.

Is this arangement Mark's own or should we trace it back to Jesus himself? Surely we have to agree that the episode at Caesarea Philippi was important in the unfolding of Jesus' ministry. But it is questionable how well it serves its purpose as a pivotal point in his mission. Peter confesses Jesus as Messiah but completely misunderstands his role as Suffering Servant. As for Jesus' proclamation of the kingdom, it would be unconvincing to insist that he spent all his energy proclaiming the arrival of the kingdom before Caesarea Philippi, with hardly a word about entering it until after that event. The two dimensions, arrival and entry, are inseparable. The kingdom of God has come, and it is of greatest urgency for men to accept and enter it. Even in the Synoptics outline there is no strict adherence to the division. Entering the kingdom is at least implicit in Mark 4:11 and the Q sayings, Luke 6:20, 7:28.

The arrangement of sayings "before" and "after" Caesarea Philippi, then, is a literary device employed for a theological purpose. This is not surprising, for the evangelists have impressive flexibility and creativity in their arrangements of sayings and stories. But why here?

That is not difficult to answer. The evangelists want to make the point that proclamation precedes acceptance. The kingdom cannot be entered until it has come. That it *has* come is of first importance. Let us make that point first, say the writers of the Gospels, then make use of Jesus' sayings about entering the kingdom to show the kind of response that is needed.

Let us examine these two groups of sayings as they stand in contrast.

1. *Mark*

  a. The kingdom of God has come

    1:15 "The kingdom of God is upon you" (NEB; cf. Matt. 4:17).

    4:11 "To you has been given the secret of the kingdom of God" (Matt. 13:11; Luke 8:10).

4:26 "The kingdom of God is as if a man should scatter seed upon the ground."

4:30, 31 "With what can we compare the kingdom of God . . . ? It is like a grain of mustard seed . . . " (Matt. 13:31; Luke 13:18 f.).

9:1 "Truly, I say to you, there are some standing here who will not taste death before they see the kingdom of God come with power" (Matt. 16:28; Luke 9:27).

b. On receiving and entering the kingdom

9:47 "It is better for you to *enter* the kingdom of God with one eye than with two eyes to be thrown into hell" (cf. Matt. 18:9).

10:14 "Let the children come to me, do not hinder them; for to such *belongs* the kingdom of God" (Matt. 19:14; Luke 18:16).

10:15 "Truly, I say to you, whoever does not *receive* the kingdom of God like a child shall not enter it" (Matt. 18:3; Luke 18:17).

10:23 "How hard it will be for those who have riches to *enter* the kingdom of God" (Matt. 19:23; Luke 18:24).

10:24 "Children, how hard it is to *enter* the kingdom of God."

10:25 "It is easier for a camel to go through the eye of a needle than for a rich man to *enter* the kingdom of God" (Matt. 19:24; Luke 18:25).

12:34 To the scribe: "You are not *far from* the kingdom of God."

14:25 "Truly, I say to you, I shall not drink again of the fruit of the vine until that day when I drink it new *in* the kingdom of God" (Matt. 26:29; Luke 22:18).

2. The Q material. The division in Q is similar but not so well balanced as in Mark.

a. The kingdom of God has come

The first two sayings do not fit the pattern exactly since they imply both the presence and possession of the kingdom.

83

Luke 6:20; Matt. 5:3 "Blessed are you poor (Matthew: poor in spirit), for yours is the kingdom of God" (Matthew: heaven).

Luke 7:28; Matt. 11:11 "Yet he who is least in the kingdom of God is greater than he" (sc. John the Baptist).

Luke 10:9; Matt. 10:7 "The kingdom of God has come near to you."

Luke 10:11; Matt. 10:14 "Nevertheless know this, that the kingdom of God has come near."

Luke 11:20; Matt. 12:28 "But if it is by the finger (Matthew: Spirit) of God that I cast out demons, then the kingdom of God has come upon you."

b. On receiving and entering the kingdom

Luke 12:31; Matt. 6:33 "Instead, seek his kingdom, and these things shall be *yours* as well.

Next come the "entering" sayings of "Special Matthew" (M) and "Special Luke" (L).

3. The M material.

5:10 "Blessed are those who are persecuted for righteousness' sake, for *theirs* is the kingdom of heaven."

5:20 "For I tell you, unless your righteousness exceeds that of the scribes and Pharisees, you will never *enter* the kingdom of heaven."

7:21 "Not every one who says to me, 'Lord, Lord,' shall *enter* the kingdom of heaven, but he who does the will of my Father who is in heaven."

18:3 f. "Truly, I say to you, unless you turn and become like children, you will never *enter* the kingdom of heaven. Whoever humbles himself like this child, he is the greatest *in* the kingdom of heaven."

21:31 "Truly, I say to you, the tax collectors and the harlots *go into* the kingdom of God before you."

21:43 "Therefore I tell you [sc. Pharisees], the kingdom of God will be *taken away* from you and *given* to a nation producing the fruits of it."

84

23:13 "But woe to you, scribes and Pharisees, hypocrites! because you *shut* the kingdom of heaven against men; for you neither *enter* yourselves, nor allow those who would *enter* to go in."

25:34 "Then the King will say to those at his right hand, 'Come, O blessed of my Father, *inherit* the kingdom prepared for you from the foundation of the world."

4. The L material.

12:32 "Fear not, little flock, for it is your Father's good pleasure to *give* you the kingdom."

22:28-30 "You are those who have continued with me in my trials; as my Father appointed a kingdom for me, so do I *appoint* for you, that you may eat and drink at my table *in* my kingdom, and sit on thrones judging the twelve tribes of Israel."

Accordingly, the kingdom is appointed for Jesus' disciples, is given, inherited, and received. And it can also be closed and taken away.

But how do we receive the gift of the kingdom? And what is it? An answer to the last question will clarify the first one. The kingship of God is his creative activity in every dimension of human existence. He is seeking to persuade us to follow his way of wholeness. The kingdom is "re-presented" to us in the person of Jesus who embodies divine wholeness in his words and deeds. Therein lies the profundity of the incarnation. God is "in Jesus," calling us into his way, the way of creative fidelity. Accordingly, the ministry of Jesus is a ministry of persuasion, not of violence. It is a ministry that awakens us out of sleep, reminding us that the wakefulness of existence lies in the unity of the self, which in turn lies in the being of God. To be is to be together; *esse est co-esse;* to be is to be whole. Jesus ministers to the fragmented, the estranged, the sinful, the sick.

He adamantly opposes men's insistence on a world of separateness, sundered apart by an overweening pride that creates two social castes—the acceptable and the unacceptable. The kingdom reverses this standard. Let those who deny creative wholeness by their rejection of the socially unacceptable know that it is they who judge themselves before the justice of God.

The central thrust of Jesus' attack on the religionists is aimed at their lack of integrity. They refuse to stand behind their words. They make pious claims, but fail to come through, to act compassionately. For this reason, they lack integrity. They are destructive forces in the world. They are in league with the demonic powers that make men legion instead of one. They split men apart, destroying their relations with themselves, with other men, and with God. That is why the kingdom of God is opposed to all demonic destructiveness that tears men from themselves and from others. The reign of God comes and continues to come as the divine creativity that realizes God's eternal desire for the sociality of his creation. Wholeness, unity, creative fidelity—these are the gifts of the kingdom.

How, then, do we receive these gifts of grace and enter into the divine process of renewal? Jesus speaks often of faith and of becoming like little children. We are to begin with the belief that existence *is this way,* and in the living of this belief come to know the fecundity of these gifts. The kingdom of God belongs to the little child (Mark 10:14); it cannot be entered without that kind of faith (Mark 10:15; cf. Matt. 18:3 f.). It is only when we pray with the faith expressed by "Abba, Father," as Jesus prayed (Mark 14:36), that we come to know God and his creativity among men. Only then do we understand what it may cost us in suffering as well as joy if we pursue the life of wholeness. "Abba" was an intimate word, full of love and intimacy as well as awe and respect, used by a little child addressing his father. Jesus tells us that to enter the kingdom we must "become little again" before God. Before his coming, never had anyone in the whole history of Jewish literature addressed God so familiarly. Unless we can learn to say "Abba" like little children (Matt. 18:3 f.), we cannot enter the kingdom of God.[10]

In philosophical language, Michael Polanyi makes the same point about faith and knowledge. Faith is not only the way of the kingdom, it is the way of knowing anything at all. We must believe before we can understand. Somewhere we have to say, I believe: I believe in this body of truth, or in this society of learned men, in this way of looking at things, or in this scientific method. Epistemology begins and ends with commitment, belief, and trust. Polanyi rests his case on the Augustinian formula that all knowledge derives from an antecedent gift of grace, received in belief: *nisi credideritis, non intelligitis.*[11] In epistemological studies, twentieth-century man is reawakening to the truth that belief is the source of all knowledge. For too long that fundamental fact of existence has been forgotten.

It is hitting the mark squarely to describe Jesus' ministry as a fiduciary mission. To know God and his wholeness is to *believe* in his wholeness and his primordial longing for the wholeness of all creation. To know God, to enter his kingdom, is to believe that in every word and act of wholeness he is present in creative power (recall the parables of the good Samaritan and of the waiting father). To say "Abba, Father" is to believe in this kind of world; it is to make our decisions and to take up our responsibilities with the quality of intentionality in which past, present, and future are God's. Only then are we freed from Legion to become whole again.

Faith and knowledge, then, are inseparable. Faith and the kingdom are inseparable. Faith and wholeness are inseparable. We enter the kingdom when we believe that God is present in every act of creative fidelity; we enter it when we *intend* the world in this way and desire its reconciliation in his image. Jesus' focus upon the art of personal wholeness, including his use of ordinary episodes to illustrate it, destroys the false dichotomy between the sacred and the profane. His witness is, "The kingdom of God is in the midst of you." There are tremendous implications in this for the understanding of human existence.

READINGS ON CHAPTER THREE

Beare, Frank W. *The Earliest Records of Jesus.* New York: Abingdon Press, 1962.
Davies, W. D. *The Setting of the Sermon on the Mount.* Cambridge: Cambridge University Press, 1964.
Hunter, A. M. *Design for Life: An Exposition of the Sermon on the Mount.* London: SCM Press, 1954.
Jeremias, Joachim. *The Parables of Jesus.* Translated by S. H. Hooke. London: SCM Press, 1963.
————. *The Sermon on the Mount.* Translated by Norman Perrin. Philadelphia: Fortress Press, 1963.
McArthur, Harvey K. *Understanding the Sermon on the Mount.* New York: Harper & Row, 1960.
Marcel, Gabriel. *Creative Fidelity.* Translated by Robert Rosthal. New York: Noonday Press, 1964.
Perrin, Norman. *The Kingdom of God in the Teaching of Jesus.* London: SCM Press, 1963.
————. *Rediscovering the Teaching of Jesus.* New York: Harper & Row, 1967.
Polanyi, Michael. *Personal Knowledge: Towards a Post-Critical Philosophy.* Harper Torchbooks; New York: Harper & Row, 1964.
————. *Science, Faith and Society.* Chicago: Phoenix Books, 1964.
Tödt, Heinz Eduard. *The Son of Man in the Synoptic Tradition.* Translated by Dorothea M. Barton. Philadelphia: Westminster Press, 1965.

CHAPTER FOUR

The
Kingdom of God
and the
Son of Man

IN THE LAST CHAPTER, when examining the sabbath-saying "The Son of man is lord even of the sabbath" (Mark 2:28), it was noted that "Son of man" and "kingdom of God" find a common center in Jesus. The task in this chapter will be to try out this theory and to see whether or not "Son of man" is also a periphrasis for Jesus' personal pronoun "I," as it is for the kingdom of God.

The Son of man sayings are rather more difficult to unravel because their precise meaning is not always clear. It is beyond any reasonable doubt that Jesus used the title in almost as favorite a manner as he did kingdom of God. The fact that both phrases virtually disappear in the apostolic writings suggests that they were original with Jesus, for the church would hardly have created terms it no longer used in its Christology. The early church dropped these veiled self-references of Jesus because they recognized him as the embodiment of God's reign and the Son of man, and no longer needed to employ these metaphors. Instead of proclaiming the kingdom and the Son of man, they proclaimed Christ himself. The mystery of Jesus' ministry was now unveiled, and the meaning of his historical person raised to historic and cosmic significance in the titles "Christ," "Lord," and "Logos."

But in what sense did Jesus use "Son of man," and how many of the sayings are genuinely his? The utterances themselves may be classified under three headings: first, sayings concerning his present status; second, his imminent suffering, death, and resurrection; and third, his future coming.

The Future Coming of Jesus

There is least disagreement over the genuineness of the third group. Heinz Tödt, a second generation Bultmannian scholar, recognizes a number of these utterances as being Jesus' own. It is always good to begin where there is agreement, so let us look at each of these genuine sayings in turn. They all have similar characteristics. First, they are free of bizarre apocalyptic. Jesus' teaching is eschatological and emerges from the apocalyptic tradition rather than the rabbinical tradition, but it never indulges itself in the curious "signs of the times" peculiar to radical apocalyptic. Second, the sayings combine the themes of promise and warning, so typical of Jesus' teaching in general. They present men with a choice: either to be faithful to Jesus' proclamation and receive the promise of the future or to reject him and incur judgment. Accordingly, Jesus does not overtly proclaim his messiahship but gives emphasis to the responsibility of his hearers to decide. Again, it is the present response of men which decides the future. If they accept the promise of God's future, they are freed to live in the present.[1]

Tödt's first group is comprised of the comparison sayings: "For as the lightning comes from the east and shines as far as the west, so will be the coming of the Son of man" (Matt. 24:27; Luke 17:24, Q); "As were the days of Noah, so will be the coming of the Son of man. [For as in those days before the flood they were eating and drinking, marrying and giving in marriage, until the day when Noah entered the ark,] and they did not know until the flood came and swept them all away, so will be the coming of the Son of man" (Matt. 24:37, 39; Luke 17:26, Q); ["Likewise as it was in the days of Lot —they ate, they drank, they bought, they sold, they planted, they built, but on the day when Lot went out from Sodom fire and brimstone rained from heaven and destroyed them all —] so will it be on the day when the Son of man is revealed" (Luke 17:30).

The second is the sign—or menace—saying: "For as Jonah became a sign to the men of Nineveh, so will the Son of man be to this generation" (Luke 11:30).

The third is the warning saying: "Therefore you also must be ready; for the Son of man is coming at an hour you do not expect" (Matt. 24:44; Luke 12:40, Q).

Finally, we have a set of promise sayings: "And I tell you, every one who acknowledges me before men, the Son of man also will acknowledge before the angels of God; but he who denies me before men will be denied before the angels of God" (Luke 12:8 f.; Matt. 10:32 f., Q). Essentially the same saying appears in Mark 8:38 and its parallels: "For whoever is ashamed of me and of my words in this adulterous and sinful generation, of him will the Son of man also be ashamed."

Now the remarkable characteristic of these sayings is that they maintain the tension between the present and future, which is so typical of Jesus' teaching. No signs are given except the signs of Noah, Lot, and Jonah who symbolize wasted days, the breakdown of human relationships, and unconcern for the divine dimension of existence. The stories warn of imminent judgment; every moment is an eschatological present in which the future may be won or lost. The future may be captured by a positive response to divine grace, as it is in the tale about Nineveh's repentance, or it may be lost as quickly as the coming of flood, earthquake, fire, and lightning: "The Son of man is coming at an hour you do not expect" (Matt. 24:44).

We simply cannot dismiss this futurist teaching of Jesus as some vestige of first-century apocalyptic which turned out to be wrong. As a matter of fact, it is as relevant now as it was then. Every moment has a finality about it. The authentic man is conscious of the judgment of the future and its promises upon every word he speaks, every act he performs, every decision he makes. He lives into the future—he exists, stands beyond himself, lives not just for the moment, but lives out the present *sub specie aeternitatis,* under the future which belongs to God.

Now Jesus does not predict the time of the coming of judgment and fulfillment. He does not claim to know the day or hour (Mark 13:32). He simply proclaims its coming, setting up an exhilarating eschatological tension between "we are" and "we shall be."

This tension between present and future requires careful thought. If there is one aspect of Jesus' teaching that has been most misinterpreted, it is his understanding of the future. Was he an apocalyptic fanatic? Did he negate the world and the importance of the present moment for some otherworldly kingdom? Did he go to the cross mistaken about his mission and in error about the end of the world he claimed would come in his lifetime? Did historic Christianity perpetuate the error of its founder by negating the present for the yet-to-come? These are questions that are honestly asked, and all too often answered affirmatively. Christianity is then dismissed. Albert Camus is an example of the contemporary non-theist who sees a serious weakness in this strain of Christian eschatology.

Camus has been critical of historic Christianity for what he calls its overemphasis on "we shall be" and its neglect of "we are." Like pragmatic political ideologies, historic Christianity has been prone to slight the values of the present and overlook wrongs to be righted, and to lose itself in the dream of a better world to come. The exponents of pragmatic political philosophy have dreamed a worldly dream of an earthly utopia to be won through the inexorable dialectic of history. They have not stopped at murder to achieve that goal. But Christians have also murdered, Camus says, indirectly, by forsaking the present for the heaven to come, patiently suffering the ills of the world in ascetic contemplation. Man cries out for justice, and Christianity responds with the proclamation of the kingdom, eternal life, and the necessity of faith. Christianity postpones the cure of evil and murder to a point beyond history, while the masses cry out for justice. But we cannot wait, writes Camus; our place is by their side, without the God of Christianity. It is the "now," not the "to come," that demands our allegiance.[2]

Christianity has discovered an eloquent critic in Camus, that sensitive man who brought his own lightning judgment upon the failures of the church. It is a criticism almost as devastating as Jesus' attack on the unwholeness of established religion in his own day, although we must remember that Camus attacks Christianity because he does not believe it is true, while Jesus criticizes a perversion of true religion.

Here we must pause to reflect. Jesus the critic was also Jesus the affirmer, whose mission was to fulfill, not to destroy: "Think not that I have come to abolish the law and the prophets; I have come not to abolish them but to fulfill them" (Matt. 5:17). Camus certainly cannot mean to proscribe Christianity *in toto*. Not every Christian has sacrificed the "we are" for the "we shall be." Indeed, Western history since Christian beginnings has been predominantly an incarnational culture with its heart in the present. Western man has felt the tension between present and future, and because he has genuinely believed in a future of promise he has realized unparalleled accomplishments in the present. Our culture is thoroughly eschatological, with its roots deep in Christian eschatology.

Camus does not write, either, as one who is entirely devoid

of futurity. He speaks of human existence in words that reflect his Christian heritage and echo the commitment of Jesus. He writes of a renaissance beyond these present ruins and nihilism, of an inevitable light at the end of our tunnel of darkness. Camus has his own futurism, his own "we shall be."[3] But it is a futurism that is given to the present: "Real generosity toward the future lies in giving all to the present."[4] What a magnificent sentence that is! It is a great affirmation of faith. And when Camus describes our giving all to the present, he speaks in familiar phrases of a strange form of love— living for the humiliated, rebelling against the absurdities of evil and injustice by renouncing life in love, without resentment, rancor, malice, or tyranny. He describes the radiant joy of loving life and believing in living man and in the things of the world.[5]

But how is this different from the language of Jesus? Camus cannot help using the incarnational language of Christianity which proclaims an identical love, sacrifice, radiance, joy, and hope in the present of living men. That radiant, joyful affirmation of the world and the present goes back to the first Hebrew story of creation, to God's witness to the goodness of the world. And it is reiterated in the person of Jesus, that consummate historical incarnation of "the rebel" who has a limit under the sun, the limit of love and justice and oneness with the oppressed and humiliated.

Were the Son of man sayings to convince us that the major thrust of Jesus' message was toward the future rather than the present, then perhaps we might call the relevance of his ministry into question. Yet, just as Camus cannot do without a future that ennobles the present by giving it focus and meaning, so the ministry of Jesus is directed to the present in full view of the future. *The future will be what we choose to make it*. It is what we decide upon now that is important. Live, then, a life of which you will not be ashamed. Act with the full responsibility of action alone, with awareness that it is your act, that it has your signature upon it and can be claimed in your name.

That is what Jesus is saying when he talks about the coming of the Son of man. Live *now* the life of wholeness, the life of integrity. Let there be no question of your being called into question: "I tell you, every one who acknowledges me before men, the Son of man also will acknowledge before the angels of God" (Luke 12:8).

Every act has an ultimate significance. This belief ennobles human existence and bestows upon it the quality of sacrament. Every word, every act is to be lived in the presence of the wholeness of Jesus. That is the important element in these Son of man sayings. Faithfulness is to Jesus himself, to his personal embodiment of wholeness in the present.

But this being the case it seems to us premature to dismiss as unauthentic all the other Son of man utterances. If we are judged by the Son of man in view of our response to the person of Jesus, how are we to distinguish the two?

This question confronts us with the essential issue of Jesus' attitude, and his understanding of his mission. There can no longer be any doubt that Jesus' attitude is recoverable in his words and acts. He assumes the prerogatives of a new Moses by placing his own words in antithesis to the Torah ("But I say"), therefore proving himself more than a rabbi. He shatters the letter of the law by calling into question the attitude to the sabbath commandment. He breaks down the classical distinction between the sacred and the secular by stressing the purity and freedom of the heart of man. He destroys the concept of a world in which man is controlled by demonic powers, and he announces that the kingdom of God has come to remove this threat. He proclaims that the time must be lived without anxiety. He announces that the kingdom of God is present and already suffering abuse from its opponents since the days of John. And he believes himself full of the Spirit of God when he uses the remarkable word amen at the beginning of important sayings, and dispels the demonic in the Spirit's name. (In the expectation of Judaism, the Spirit of God was to be a gift of the end time.)

All these evidences are adduced by Ernst Käsemann[6] to reveal Jesus' attitude toward his mission. He is ready to speak of Jesus' belief: "It was the belief of Jesus that, in his word, the *basileia* was coming to his hearers." Yet, he cannot bring himself to admit of Jesus' messianic consciousness:

Does this mean that he understood himself to be the Messiah? The only way of dealing briefly with this question is simply to express at this point one's own personal opinion. I personally am convinced that there can be no possible grounds for answering this question in the affirmative. I consider all passages in which any kind of Messianic prediction occurs to be kerygma shaped by the community.[7]

Here is a refreshing honesty, revealing the fiduciary nature of critical analysis. Käsemann is a more radical critic than most and plays the salutary role of reminding us how the early community shaped the sayings of Jesus around their impressions of his risen person.

Yet, something seems not quite right with his skepticism. I can be skeptical, yes, about the overt messianic predictions which have been inserted by the community (the other Son of man sayings will be looked at shortly), although no one can be absolutely certain of that either. But I wonder how he can admit to so much that is messianic in the attitude of Jesus (the list of "authentic" material above) without coming to the conclusion that Jesus was conscious of being the Messiah. When he admits that Jesus uses language appropriate to the end, when he concludes that Jesus assumed unheard-of prerogatives in setting himself above Moses, how can he avoid the direct implication that Jesus was conscious of his messianic mission? What more does one have to do to evince messiahship? If Jesus' language and behavior is un-messianic, what does it mean to be the Messiah?

There is a certain naïveté in Käsemann's analysis, or perhaps it would be better to say that there is a serious misunderstanding of what it means to be a person underlying his admission, on the one hand, that Jesus' attitude is tied up with messianic claims and, on the other, that he did not understand himself to be the Messiah. Persons cannot be fractured into compartments. We cannot say that a person has a certain consciousness of his mission and at the same time does not know what he is about. When a person speaks in a certain manner and behaves in another, we conclude that he is untrustworthy and does not know who he is or what he is doing.

But Jesus' words and acts are impressively integral, and we trust those sayings we judge to be authentically his as revelatory of his person. When Jesus uses the personal pronoun "I" ("But *I* say to you," "Amen, *I* say to you") he stands in back of every word with personal fidelity and personal intentionality. If his words and acts are messianic in character, *it is because he intends them to be,* and if he intends them to be, he is thinking of himself in messianic terms.

When Käsemann claims that there can be no possible grounds for affirmatively answering the question of Jesus' messianic consciousness, he is voicing a position that has created the greatest confusion in New Testament studies since the time of Bultmann. He is assuming, with others in the Bultmannian school, that a man's word can be separated from his intention. This preoccupation with "word," as divorced from the person who utters the word, has permitted the Bultmannians to center their theology in words *about* Jesus (the Gospel According to John and the Pauline Epistles) rather than in the words *of* Jesus. Here is the greatest irony: In their concern for knowledge *of* God rather than knowledge *about* God, they have actually focused upon the Word which is Christ, an abstraction, and forsaken the personal concretion of the Word of God in Jesus himself.

Later Bultmannian scholars, like Käsemann, still distinguish between the word of Jesus and the self-consciousness of Jesus, between Jesus' understanding of existence and his self-understanding.[8] All such talk is untrue to an analysis of language and persons. Words are meaningful only when they are spoken in good faith, and that means that no genuine understanding of existence can emerge from the words of someone who does not personally embody the meaning of those words in his behavior. In his later writings, particularly in the *Philosophical Investigations,* Ludwig Wittgenstein made this point emphatically.[9] Speech involves an "I" behind the words. Language is meaningful only when we personally *intend* it to be so. Every word must be signed by the signature of the speaker.

Everywhere in the Gospels Jesus is witnessed to as a person of wholeness, not as one who merely voiced words and failed to back them up with appropriate intention and behavior. Were the latter true, so much the worse for the historical Jesus. But we cannot have it both ways. Either Jesus embodied the Word of God in his life, or he was a man of bad faith and mere gesture.

This little excursus into the question of Jesus' personal intention has brought us to a point of decision about the genuineness of the remaining Son of man sayings. If Käsemann rejects them all because he is personally of the opinion that Jesus was never intentionally the Messiah, then his decision rests upon a false separation between words and the intentional person who speaks them. If the body of sayings Käsemann himself acknowledges to be genuine are accepted as such, one is led to the logical conclusion that Jesus was conscious of his messianic role and that he intended his words and his acts to be messianic. This personal belief comes from an existentialist analysis of what it means to be a person, and there the case must rest.

The question, therefore, is not whether Jesus was conscious of being the Messiah. The question is how he understood his messiahship. When the inquiry is shifted to this level, the mystery of his mission is to be understood in the *nature* of his messiahship. The nature of his mission was that as the Son of man he was to suffer and die—alone. The disciples were unprepared for his suffering the cross alone with no observable evidence of victory. After what had happened to John the Baptist, Jesus and his disciples were certainly prepared for suffering. And if the Son of man teaching was understood against the background of Daniel 7:13-14, 18, they anticipated the corporate triumph of the "saints of the Most High," and were willing to suffer corporately to win that victory. But the enigma of the title of Son of man lay in Jesus' fusion of corporate triumph with the Suffering Servant theme of Isaiah 53. It was this motif the disciples failed to intuit correctly. Which brings us to the second group of Son of man sayings.

The Ministry of Jesus

The "not yet" language which Tödt accepts as genuine in one group of sayings has already been examined. Another group, the "now" sayings, reveal Jesus' intention to fulfill the meaning of Son of man in his ministry.

1. The first important saying is "the Son of man has authority on earth to forgive sins" (Mark 2:10; Matt. 9:6; Luke 5:24). It is possible to interpret the whole section between the phrase "he said to the paralytic," of Mark 2:5, and its repetition in Mark 2:10 as an addition of the community which changes the original miracle story to a defense of the church's authorization to forgive sins. That is the position of F. W. Beare.[10] However, he is of the opinion that Jesus never used the term Son of man as a title but only as a simple surrogate for the personal pronoun "I," and that the community elevated it to the level of the title "Messiah."[11] It is not surprising, then, that he takes a negative view of the Son of man sayings in general.

The interpretation of the sayings suggested here rests upon

the belief that the term is not just a surrogate for "I," but a title which Jesus intentionally and creatively used to refer to his ministry in the indirect manner typical of his parables and the metaphor "kingdom of God." The mystery of his person has to be seen through the unity of his language and works, not through theological terms alone.

We must not allow the parenthetical form of the story of the paralytic to throw us off guard and force us to assume too hastily that it is a polemical insertion of the early church. We first ought to ask ourselves: Is the unheard-of prerogative of forgiving sins in keeping with the intentionality of Jesus elsewhere? The answer is clearly yes. If he assumes a position of authority over Moses and the Torah, as Käsemann argues so well, Jesus goes even further to assume what is God's prerogative, that of forgiving sinners. It is this that lies behind his controversy with the scribes and Pharisees. Jesus' parables proclaim that the divine love of forgiveness and healing has come in his words and deeds. He has come to find the lost (the three parables of Luke 15 concerning the lost sheep, the lost coin, and the prodigal son) and to inaugurate the messianic feast, which is the symbol of the most intimate fellowship with God (Matt. 8:11; Mark 2:15 ff.; Luke 14:16 ff.; Matt. 22:1 ff.) There is no question but that Jesus is embodying what is the prerogative of God, as Bornkamm also assumes.[12]

This being the case, it is likely that Mark 2:10 preserves an original saying of Jesus. Agreeing with his opponents that only God can forgive sins, he declares that God is present in his own authority to forgive; that is, God is present in his person.[13] Hence, the charge of blasphemy (Mark 2:7). Jesus is more than a prophet. He personifies the divine presence in its healing activity: "Those who are well have no need of a physician, but those who are sick; I came not to call the righteous, but sinners" (Mark 2:17 and para.).

2. The saying at the end of the cornfield episode, "The Son of man is lord even of the sabbath" (Mark 2:28), is

consistent with the language of Jesus in general. He assumes a station above the law, which is the very prerogative of God.

3. A final "now" saying will serve to introduce the second category, the "suffering" utterances. In answering the promise of the scribe, "Teacher, I will follow you wherever you go," Jesus replies, "Foxes have holes, and birds of the air have nests; but the Son of man has nowhere to lay his head" (Matt. 8:20; Luke 9:58, Q). Here is a saying that is a periphrasis for "I," reiterates the presence of the Son of man, yet is simultaneously an indirect prediction of Jesus' suffering. The phrase "nowhere to lay his head" symbolizes the suffering role of Jesus as he faces rejection. As Son of man, Jesus personally incorporates the "saints of the Most High" of Daniel and the Suffering Servant of Isaiah 53. He individualizes and concretizes these eschatological figures, as he embodies the kingship of God in his person. The Son of man and the kingdom of God are metaphors with many identical dimensions, and they find their *locus* in Jesus. He claims them both with an indirectness, even detachment, because of the nature of his mission; they are his not simply through a verbal claim, but in the wholeness of the life he intentionally lives.

Sayings About the Passion

The last group is made up of sayings that anticipate the suffering of the Son of man. Except for the Q saying, "The Son of man has nowhere to lay his head," all of the suffering utterances are either in Mark or Luke. It is not surprising that Q makes no explicit references to the suffering Son of man, since it was not a gospel but a general collection of Jesus' sayings and hence contained no passion narrative.

Now a glance at the five prophecies of the passion in Mark's narrative reveals details which are very likely expansions added after the event by the community. But we have to be patient not to excuse the whole group of sayings too quickly, for if the suspected additions are excepted and the remainder placed in italics, there appears a body of suffering predictions startlingly like Isaiah 53:[14]

"The Son of man *must suffer many things, and be rejected* by the elders and the chief priests and the scribes, *and be killed,* and after three days rise again" (Mark 8:31).

[It is] "written of the Son of man, *that he should suffer many things and be treated with contempt*" (Mark 9:12).

"The Son of man *will be delivered into the hands of men, and they will kill him; and when he is killed,* after three days he will rise" (Mark 9:31).

"The Son of man *will be delivered* to the chief priests and the scribes, and they will condemn him to death, and deliver him to the Gentiles; and they will mock him, and spit upon him, and scourge him, *and kill him;* and after three days he will arise" (Mark 10:33 f.).

"For the Son of man also *came not to be served but to serve, and to give his life as a ransom for many*" (Mark 10:45).

Let us put these italicized sayings together: The Son of man must suffer many things, and be rejected and treated with contempt, and be delivered into the hands of men, who will kill him. The Son of man came not to be served but to serve, and to give his life as a ransom for many.

The fact that almost every one of these phrases appears to reflect the Hebrew text of Isaiah 53 leaves little doubt that Jesus was well acquainted with the Isaianic Suffering Servant, and intentionally used Isaiah's passion-language because he understood his mission as one who must suffer for the many. When we keep in mind that the Son of man in Daniel 7 is a figure who represents the saints of the Most High, the similarities of individuality and corporateness in the Son of man and the Suffering Servant are impressive. Since the early church does not use the title "Son of man" outside the Synoptics (the same is generally true of the kingdom of God), we are led to the conclusion that it was Jesus' own creative choice which explains its appearance in the Gospels. Moreover, the theme of redemption is so strong in Jesus' teaching, and his ministry so deeply indebted to the heritage of the Old Testament, that it would be surprising if he were to make no allusions to the passages in Second Isaiah which speak of the Suffering Servant and his ministry of suffering for the many.

Is Luke's account then totally editorial when he has Jesus standing up to read Isaiah in the synagogue at Nazareth (Luke 4:16-21)?

The Spirit of the Lord is upon me,
> because he has anointed me to preach good news to the poor.

He has sent me to proclaim release to the captives
and recovering of sight to the blind,
to set at liberty those who are oppressed,
> to proclaim the acceptable year of the Lord.

—Luke 4:18 f.; cf. Isaiah 61:1 f.; 58:6

Perhaps. But in view of Jesus' understanding of the new age and his ministry to the poor and afflicted, it is more than likely that he reflected upon these passages and employed them in his proclamation of the kingdom of God. "Today this scripture has been fulfilled in your hearing" (Luke 4:21): that is the constant theme of his words and acts. His ministry is to the sick and the outcast: "For the Son of man came to seek and to save the lost" (Luke 19:10). It is this mission to the lost which is integrally related to his suffering. He suffers with the lost because of his compassion for them, and he suffers on behalf of the lost because of the opposition he encounters in seeking them and making them whole again.

This double sense of suffering (suffering with and suffering for) is related to the whole of his ministry from beginning to end, and it is succinctly expressed in the saying found in Luke

12:49 f.: "I came to cast fire upon the earth; and would that it were already kindled! I have a baptism to be baptized with; and how I am constrained until it is accomplished!" Here is no Hellenistic, gnosticizing Christianity intruding itself into the language of Jesus, but rather a metaphorical reference to his suffering, which is so characteristic of his work and words. The "fire" is the fire of divine proclamation as we find it in the prophetic tradition. Yahweh says to Jeremiah, "Behold, I am making my words in your mouth a fire" (Jer. 5:14), and the prophet cries, "There is in my heart as it were a burning fire," which he cannot hold in (Jer. 20:9). He has to speak out. But in proclaiming the word of Yahweh he suffers, both for his people and from his people as they denounce and reject him (Jer. 20:10).

Jesus understands his ministry as a baptism of suffering. He comes to reconcile the world of men, but as long as there are those who refuse the new time and insist on dividing men into the acceptable and the unacceptable, he will encounter their opposition. When he proclaims the now of the acceptable year of the Lord, which brings healing to the poor, the blind, and the oppressed, he will suffer the rejection of those who divide men into the sacred and profane. He will suffer until he is able to awaken them from their long sleep of forgetfulness, and persuade them to receive the gift of the kingdom, which is an awakening to wholeness.

The themes of suffering and corporateness are bound together in the Son of man. The prophetic theme of a suffering life identified with God's people (Isa. 53), and the apocalyptic theme of the coming corporateness of God and the saints of the Most High (Dan. 7), are combined in Jesus' understanding of the Son of man. The dimensions of time are identical to his parabolic and other eschatological language. The same tension exists between the present activity of the Son of man, his suffering ministry, and his future coming to judge and fulfill. Always, though he does not overtly make this claim,

Jesus emerges as the central figure of the kingdom. We cannot help coming to terms with him—not simply with his words, but with the whole of his person. To mean anything, words must be integral with acts. Thus, we stand before Jesus, the word and the act, and are judged by his wholeness: "And I tell you, every one who acknowledges me before men, the Son of man also will acknowledge before the angels of God; but he who denies me before men will be denied before the angels of God" (Luke 12:8 f.; Matt. 10:32 f., Q).

It is in this sense that we are to understand the incarnation of God in Jesus of Nazareth. Jesus is the *incarnate* word of God; he em-bodies the primordial will of God in his person, in his language, and in his acts and intentionality, which are inseparable. To hear Jesus speak and to see him act is to hear audibly and see visibly the proclamation of God's grace. Jesus is, as it were, transparent to God—fully visible, yet transparent to the divine creativity which encompasses human existence. That is why Jesus can sanctify the ordinary by using it as illustrative of his ministry and of God's creativity. He identifies himself with ordinary human situations in the parables, and he chooses the term "Son of man" to express his oneness with men. Little wonder that the early Christian community spoke of him as Logos, Lord, and Christ, after God had placed the divine imprimatur upon his life of wholeness. Jesus, the man of time, space, and particularity was raised to cosmic significance. He became the man for every man. Is not that the meaning of the expression "Son of man"?

READINGS ON CHAPTER FOUR

Bornkamm, Günther. *Jesus of Nazareth.* Translated by Irene and Fraser McLuskey, with James M. Robinson. New York: Harper & Row, 1960.

Camus, Albert. *The Rebel: An Essay on Man in Revolt.* Translated by Anthony Bower. New York: Vintage Books, 1962.

Fuller, Reginald H. *The Mission and Achievement of Jesus*

("Studies in Biblical Theology," No. 12.) London: SCM Press, 1954.

Käsemann, Ernst. *Essays on New Testament Themes.* Translated by W. J. Montague. ("Studies in Biblical Theology," No. 41.) London: SCM Press, 1964.

Robinson, James M. *A New Quest of the Historical Jesus* ("Studies in Biblical Theology," No. 25.) London: SCM Press, 1959.

Robinson, James M., and Cobb, John B., Jr. (eds.). *New Frontiers in Theology.* Vol. II: *The New Hermeneutic.* New York: Harper & Row, 1964.

Tödt, Heinz Eduard. *The Son of Man in the Synoptic Tradition.* Translated by Dorothea M. Barton. Philadelphia: Westminster Press, 1965.

Wittgenstein, Ludwig. *Philosophical Investigations.* Translated by G. E. M. Anscombe. Oxford: Basil Blackwell, 1958.

CHAPTER FIVE

The
Acts of the Kingdom

HAVING EXAMINED the language of Jesus, which is also the language of the kingdom, we turn to the acts of Jesus and the kingdom. One of the basic assumptions of this book is the inseparability of words and acts. And to underscore what has been said earlier, the central theme of the kingdom is that the wholeness of a person is the unity of his intentionality, speech, and acts. Thus far we have paid major attention to one aspect of Jesus' self, his language. Now our focus shifts to his works so that we may appreciate his own understanding of his unitary ministry.

Personal Acts

1. In the last chapter on the kingdom of God and the Son of man, the concluding remarks centered on the metaphorical theme of Luke 12:49 f.: "I came to cast fire upon the earth; and would that it were already kindled! I have a baptism to be baptized with; and how I am constrained until it is accomplished!" In the present chapter this motif of baptism, which so eloquently expresses the eschatological tension in the ministry of Jesus, needs to be traced from his initial baptism to his final baptism of suffering.

The baptism of Jesus is the first of many acts in which he reveals his fidelity to God and to men, in which he strikes, as it were, the tone of his ministry. As before, "act" will be used as Marcel employs it. The reality of an act is not exhausted in the visible accomplishment of a *doing*. The essence of an act is to *commit* the agent.[1] This means that when I genuinely act, I am intentionally committed to what I am doing, so that I may later lay claim to that act as my own, just as though I had signed my signature to it. A solidarity is formed between me and my act in the sense that it represents me personally, and the more it is incorporated into the totality of what I am, the more the act is mine. And the more the act is mine, the more impossible it is for me to repudiate it without denying myself.

In this analysis of what it means to be a person, Marcel has described a phenomenology of the self that is of first importance in understanding the tremendous disclosure of God in the person Jesus. The whole analysis hinges upon the distinction between genuine *act* and inauthentic *gesture*. Gesture is empty; it lacks commitment and meaning because it is anonymous. But an act always has a personal reference; it is consecrated, not in divided, discontinuous phases, but as it assumes the totality of the person who acts. In every genuine act the agent envisages a situation which involves chances, probabilities, risks, and in confronting this situation he appraises the risks and exposes himself; that is, he sets himself in a certain direction. Once he has set himself upon his personal course of action he no longer holds it as a position because he is inextricably identified with it.[2]

Here lies the very heart of Jesus' intentionality and acts, which are manifest in his baptism, the first great act of his ministry. Jesus is transparent to the presence of God because he is unified with himself; in every thing he subsequently does he is the personalization of wholeness and the relentless foe of fragmentation.

In the baptism at the river Jordan (Mark 1:9-11; cf. Matt. 3: 13-17; Luke 3:21 f.), the divine punctiliar event anticipated by the prophets of old takes on the name of Jesus of Nazareth. Christian faith has its origins in a name, a personal name, not in anonymity.

In Jesus' act of baptism, a number of lines converge upon him as though he were their personal nexus. For one, he inaugurates the new time which has begun to break in through the ministry of John the Baptist. The new time becomes an accomplished fact when God bestows his divine word of approval upon Jesus' activity. Whether the voice and vision from heaven were given to Jesus alone as a personal assurance, as in Mark's account, or were a public proclamation of the divine imprimatur placed upon him, which seems to be the case in Matthew and Luke (as well as in John 1:32-34), we are in no position to say with certainty. But Luke's description of a dove in *bodily* form, and Matthew's heavenly voice, which says *"This* is my beloved Son," suggest that the evangelists are adding public touches to what was a subjective experience of Jesus.

One thing is clear. The baptism cannot have been created by the community of faith, for Jesus' submission to John's "baptism of repentance for the forgiveness of sins" caused some embarrassment in the church. John was only a forerunner, and Jesus was believed to be without sin. How could he then have submitted to a rite of the Baptist?

Although Matthew tries to solve this problem by ascribing these words to Jesus, "Thus it is fitting for us to fulfill all righteousness" (Matt. 3:15), there is no compelling reason for us to doubt that Jesus, with all his prior training in Old Testament scripture, associated this inaugural episode with Psalm 2:7 and Isaiah 42:1. Of course this assumes that Jesus had some idea of what he was about and understood the baptism as an act of personal fidelity in which he pledged his life to God and to his people. In view of the study made earlier in this book of the language of Jesus, which shows that he consciously exercised unique, even divine, prerogatives in his teaching, it would be naïve to deny him any consciousness of his mission at the baptism.

Since Jesus made the kingdom of God a central theme of his ministry and proclaimed it in such a way that it found expression in his own words and ways, it is only fitting that he would come to understand himself through the scripture of messianic kingship, such as the following passage of Psalm 2:6 f.:

> "I have set my king
>   on Zion, my holy hill."
> I will tell of the decree of the Lord:
> He said to me, "You are my son,
>   today I have begotten you."

and the servant passage of Isaiah 42:1:

> Behold my servant, whom I uphold,
>   my chosen, in whom my soul delights;
> I have put my Spirit upon him,
>   he will bring forth justice to the nations.

Full of these messianic scriptures, Jesus went down to the river Jordan convinced that God was at work in John the Baptist. There, in an act of fidelity, he was baptized by John and consecrated his life to the Father and to the salvation of his people. In the descent of the Spirit he was anointed with *dynamis* (the divine power, Acts 10:38) that he should embody the kingship of God as a servant who must suffer for the many.

The first of Jesus' acts, then, as he inaugurates his ministry is this act of fidelity in which he purposes to assign his name to every act that follows, and to bring to his people the good news of wholeness and freedom from alienation. The filial

110

bond expressed between the Father and the Son sets the tone of his ministry of unity and fidelity.

2. In sharp contrast to the intimacy of the baptism stands the temptation (Mark 1:12 f.; Luke 4:1-13; Matt. 4:1-11, Q). Like the details of the baptism, this story is a parable of Jesus' personal experience—a story that was very likely related to the disciples after Jesus had called them together. It does not describe one episode in which Jesus confronted the tempter and defeated him once for all, but it symbolizes in imaginative, parabolic language the warfare between the dynamic of filial unity with God and the demonic forces of alienation, with which he fought to the very end (the temptation to sacrifice his fidelity was still present in Gethsemane, Mark 14:36 and para.).

Everywhere in his ministry Jesus stands opposed to the forces that make men "legion," fragmenting them and alienating them. It is striking that in the Gospel accounts the two existential possibilities for men lie cheek to jowl in starkest contrast: the unitary relation of man to God which frees one to unitary relations with others (the baptism); and the demonic appeal to break off ultimate commitments for proximate rewards which do not exist. Where Jesus' mission is to heal and make whole, the demonic leads to nihilism and estrangement. Where Jesus calls men to acts of creative fidelity, the demonic allures them to subtle enticements, first to question, then to destroy the integrity of commitment.

Every one of the three temptations in the parable illustrates the divisive allurements that lay in the path of faithfulness to the Father. The temptation to turn barren stones to bread appealed to Jesus' personal hunger: Think of yourself first. More than that, it was an appeal to provide an economic feast as a sign of the kingdom's coming, guaranteed to win a wide and popular following. But Jesus refused to give himself priority over his people, he refused to use divine miracle as magical inducement to enter the kingdom, and he rejected the appeal to make the kingdom of God a matter of economic revolution. Had he chosen that course as a subject of a Roman satellite, he would have perished by the sword as did every Zealot who rose up against Rome. If we feel a lack of economic justice in Jesus' activity which does not seem to measure up even to the message of social justice in the Old Testament prophets, let alone our own, we have to remember his contextual setting and the possibilities of his commitment. It was simply not a live option for Jesus to preach economic justice in the manner of the prophets, who were remonstrating with the ruling classes of Israel and Judah when those two states had at least a measure of autonomy left to institute reforms. As for us, we cannot forget the long parliamentary history which has made it far easier for us to correct social injustices through conscientious governmental reform.

In his political context, Jesus would have led his people to national suicide had he risen against Rome with the sword, as others perished when Jerusalem was burned and the temple leveled within forty years of his ministry. Yet Jesus' commitment to the poor is unmistakable; it is present in nearly every word and act, though the poverty he speaks of lies at a deeper level than the hunger for physical bread: "Man shall not live by bread alone." It is this word that gives us pause when we are surfeited with food and material plenty, yet still complain of hunger.

The two remaining temptations are variations on the first, for in both the tempter purposes to seduce Jesus with the reward of fame: Throw yourself down from the pinnacle of the temple—there is a sign they would come clamoring after! Use political stratagem, become an opportunist, and rule over the kingdoms of the world as Caesar rules them.

All external appeals, these. But Jesus' fidelity to the Father and to his people lay on a deeper level, at the very core of man's being: the healing of sin, pain, suffering, estrangement, anxiety, and death. The temptation parable is a signal reminder of the fidelity that characterized the acts of Jesus, and *of the agony of faithfulness;* it sets a pattern for the fidelity of his disciples whose commitment is gratefully acknowledged by Jesus because they have continued with him in his trials (Luke 22:28-30).

Corporate Acts

1. The acts of Jesus are corporate acts. His activity is characterized by disposability, in the sense in which Marcel uses the word.[3] Jesus places himself freely in the hands of others, puts himself at their disposal, and at the same time welcomes them as participants in his work.

Because his ministry is a corporate one, Jesus calls a group of twelve disciples to share in his ministry (Mark 1:16-20; Matt. 4:18-22). By this act of participation, he reveals the intersubjective nature of the kingdom that is not only the reign of God but also the realm of disciples who are "called into being" when they enter it. The disciples are now engaged in the societary work of the kingdom, preaching the good news of the gospel to the sick, the poor, the despairing: "Follow me and I will make you become fishers of men" (Mark 1:17). Nowhere else does this metaphor appear in Christian usage, inviting our confidence that it is a genuine part of the occasion on which the disciples are called to become participants in the ministry of wholeness. As a sea metaphor, it is reminiscent of what was likely the original sense of the parable of the dragnet: "The kingdom of heaven is like a net which was thrown into the sea and gathered fish of every kind" (Matt. 13:47). We cannot overestimate the importance of this societary mission, for it represents the cosmic truth that reality is social—that the divine will is to achieve the greatest degree of sociality among his creatures, as Alfred North Whitehead and Charles Hartshorne have written so articulately.[4]

2. Healing and wholeness are the full rationale of the kingdom, and it is only fitting that after the preliminary acts of personal consecration, then calling a community of co-workers, Jesus should begin to heal the sick.

Immediately we are face to face with the miracles of the kingdom, which take up nearly one third of Mark, the earliest Gospel (209 verses out of 661). They range from healings and exorcisms to resurrections and nature miracles. Are these acts of Jesus credible in part, or at all?

The "mighty acts" (*dynameis*) have been an embarrassment to some interpreters, and not only in modern times when the view of a universe enclosed by inviolable natural law ruled out their possibility (David Hume's essay on "Miracles" has become a classic statement of this school of thought). In the early period of the church, objections were voiced for radically different reasons. The Gospel According to Thomas, for instance, espoused so spiritual a Jesus that he could never have troubled himself with the evil material world, let alone with miraculous healings.

We have a right to be suspicious of reported miracles not only because most of us never experience them but also because credulous people in the history of religions have clearly let their imaginations run wild with tales of wonder. During the age of miracles in the thirteenth century, the most incredible stories are told of dead sons restored to their mothers before the image of the Blessed Virgin, of the teeth of holy men with power to confer marvelous gifts upon mortals. In the Apocryphal Infancy Gospels, unbelievable stories are related of the child Jesus, whose very bath water had power to cleanse lepers, whose sweat wrung out on the ground could make a balsam spring forth. The prodigious child himself had fantastic powers to forecast the future in detail and was not above playing tricks with his miraculous abilities, turning children into goats or withering a lad who had remonstrated

114

with him (not, however, before Jesus in a rage had called him "an insolent, godless dunderhead").[5]

Yet a word of caution. Stories of this genre were created by imaginative sects far removed from the eyewitnesses of Jesus, and they reveal a tendency to fill in gaps where little or nothing is said of Jesus in the synoptic Gospels. The dynamic acts of Jesus cannot simply be written off on principle; we cannot say that because they are often abused, miracles are therefore wholly unbelievable.

In the Gospels themselves, healings and exorcisms play a central role in Jesus' activity, and we shall look at them with an eye to understanding how they illuminate the wholeness of the kingdom. As for the inexorable laws of nature Hume wrote about, which would foreclose the whole discussion were he correct, there are few today who would not plump instead for an inexhaustible and many-dimensioned world of which we actually know very little. What we call "laws" (a rather misleading word, really), are more on the order of descriptions of certain dimensions of reality than prescriptions of what always and everywhere must occur in the universe.

Of course, that is only to say that miracles *may* be a dimension of reality as yet unexplored by most of us. It does not claim that miracles *do* happen. But at least the question is open rather than closed, as it was with Hume. The question now is, What are we to make of the witnesses to Jesus' miraculous acts?

Let us take the hard ones first, the exorcisms. Most of us find it difficult to believe in a world populated by demons; and it does not seem that Jesus believed in that kind of world either. On the contrary, the intention in his acts of exorcism is directed toward freeing the hearts of men from the terror of living in a bedeviled world. He releases them from the curse of a metaphysical dualism with its classical demonology. He rejects this dualism because of its failure to place responsibility in the heart of man rather than in the mysterious evil powers of the universe.[6] Perhaps Jesus is a child of his time and believes in the reality of demons, but what difference does that make? He views his mission as the *destruction* of the demonic threat, he calls men back to wholeness from their demonic fragmentation, and in giving them back to themselves returns them to personal responsibility.

It is difficult for us to imagine the fear which the devout must have felt for disincarnate spirits of demons who sought their abode in living victims. Jesus dispels this terror and associates it with the power of the kingdom of God: "But if it is by the finger (Spirit) of God that I cast out demons, then the kingdom of God has come upon you (Luke 11:20; Matt. 12:28, Q).

The result of his exorcising the demonic realm was wholeness in the lives of the healed. We recognize these cases as typical psychological maladies all too common in our own day: shouting (Mark 1:23 f.); crying out like a wild person, inflicting injury upon the self (Mark 5:5); suffering epileptic seizure, which dashes the victim down while he foams, grinds his teeth, and becomes rigid (Mark 9:18, 20); inability to speak (Luke 11:14; Matt. 9:32).

In each of these psychological illnesses Jesus effects a cure by bringing the "possessed" person back to unity. He dispels the unclean spirit from the demoniac in the synagogue at Capernaum (Mark 1:21-28; Luke 4:31-37) by rebuking the demon with the words "Be silent, and come out of him!" In the story of the Gerasene demoniac (Mark 5:1-20; Luke 8:26-39), which includes many details hardly characteristic of Jesus, brings back to his right mind the man who had had the legion he casts out "legion" who is many thousands of demons, and (Mark 5:8, 15).

The importance of prayer and intercession in the exorcisms is clear in the story about the healing of the epileptic child (Mark 9:14-29 and para.). The father intercedes on behalf of his son, evidences belief and a desire for greater belief ("I believe; help my unbelief!" Mark 9:24). Jesus also attributes to prayer his power to heal (Mark 9:29), which bears out the truth that the powers of the kingdom can be called forth where there is prayerful belief; but without it, the kingdom remains hidden and its healing power inaccessible (Mark 6:5). And that is true of all the acts of the kingdom. As Michael Polanyi has argued in the field of epistemology, belief is the prerequisite of every kind of knowing. "A fiduciary philosophy," he writes, "does not eliminate doubt, but (like Christianity) says that we should hold on to what we truly believe, even when realizing the absurdly remote chances of this enterprise, trusting the unfathomable intimations that call upon us to do so."[7]

Jesus' warfare is not a mere local skirmish against demons but a throwing out of the whole doctrine of demonic terror, so that men may become persons again. Those who suffer from physical illness are also called to the wholeness of the kingdom. Here the fiduciary nature of healing is remarkably clear: Jesus heals only where there is belief in his healing ability, and the list of those who find healing either by their own faith or by the faith of others is impressive: the leper (Mark 1:40), the paralytic (Mark 2:5), Jairus' daughter and the woman with the issue of blood (Mark 5:22-34), the blind man of Bethsaida (Mark 8:22-26), blind Bartimaeus (Mark 10:46-52), the centurion's servant (Luke 7:1-10; Matt. 8:5-10, 13, Q). Faith and prayer release one from fear of external forces of evil; they free a person to the power of the kingdom so that he can *act* as well as *be acted* upon. The kingdom calls men out of hopeless passivity before deterministic forces, but to be healed they must meet the freedom of the kingdom halfway with belief.

We are all well acquainted with the effectiveness of the psychosomatic approach to healing, which stresses the interactive unity of mind and body. Accordingly, we have little

117

difficulty in understanding the healing acts of Jesus, except perhaps the resurrections. But what of the nature miracles, where "even the wind and sea obey him"? These place a considerable strain on our faith, and perhaps are to be taken as parables of faith (the feeding of the multitude, the stilling of the storm, the walking on the water). On the other hand, Jesus may have possessed a remarkable power over nature which complemented the divine prerogatives he assumed in his language.

But is this problem a profitable one to pursue? The real issue comes back at last to the matter of *personal* wholeness which is preeminent in the words and works of the kingdom Jesus personifies. He refuses miraculous signs for the sake of demonstration, and heals for one reason alone: because he has compassion on those who are alienated from God and from themselves. The kingdom of God has only one enemy, the forces of legion, which are fragmentation and bad faith. These are the powers Jesus dispels in his exorcisms and healings.

There is one nature miracle that has embedded within it an especially significant act of fellowship, the feeding of the five thousand (Mark 6:30-44). The story contains several motifs that are similar to the metaphors of the messianic banquet of the kingdom. An event that immediately comes to mind is the Last Supper, during which Jesus took the bread, blessed it, broke it, and gave it to his disciples. There is a striking parallel, too, to Elisha's multiplication of twenty barley loaves to feed one hundred men (2 Kings 4:42-44; cf. John 6:9, 13), for Elisha had received a double portion of Elijah's spirit (2 Kings 2:9-14). Since Elijah was a forerunner of Jesus (Mark 9:13), Jesus would be expected to surpass them both. The arrangement of the crowd in units of fifties and hundreds reminds us of Moses' instructions that the children of Israel gather in groups of thousands, hundreds, and fifties in the exodus. Hence, there is an eschatological motif, the new exodus, which Jesus is accomplishing in this banquet of the kingdom of God.

We suspect that the incident was not originally a nature miracle at all (the account probably should conclude at Mark 6:41), but instead a fellowship meal of the kingdom. It is in any event an act in which Jesus symbolizes the unity of his people in a common meal. The picture of them all seated together with Jesus in their midst contrasts dramatically with the demon-possessed and the sick crying out in loneliness in their estrangement and sorrow.

The importance that Jesus himself accorded his ministry of healing is summarized succinctly in his reply to John the Baptist's request for his credentials, and we do well to draw our discussion of the healing acts of Jesus to a close with these words: "Go and tell John what you hear and see: the blind receive their sight and the lame walk, lepers are cleansed and the deaf hear, and the dead are raised up, and the poor have good news preached to them" (Matt. 11:4 f.; Luke 7:22 f., Q).

3. So Jesus "went about doing good and healing all that were oppressed by the devil, for God was with him" (Acts 10:38). But he did not go alone. In an acted parable he had selected twelve men (Mark 3:13 f.)—representing the twelve tribes of Israel—and sent them out to proclaim the kingdom of God (Mark 6:7-13, 30; Matt. 10:1-42; Luke 9:1-6 and a doublet, 10:1-20). The mission of the twelve was to proclaim the good news of the kingdom in word and deed. They were to go two by two, traveling light, and give their attention to preaching and healing. Matthew and Luke add that they were to announce the arrival of the reign of God: "And as you go proclaim the message: 'The kingdom of Heaven is upon you *(ēggiken)*' " (Matt. 10:7; Luke 9:2, NEB).

Accordingly, the mission in every way parallels the mission of Jesus himself: proclaiming the presence of the reign of God, exercising the powers of exorcism, healing, raising the dead. What else Jesus may have said to his disciples is not certain, for the accounts are composite and reflect the times of persecution in the early church. Much of the material in Matthew 10:17-25, for example, is drawn from the apocalyptic discourse of Mark 13, and does not harmonize at all with the tenor of a first mission charge. Here is a clear example of the freedom with which the evangelists readapted an original setting to the situation facing them at the time of their writing, for their central interest was to discover the existential relevance of Jesus' charge for their own times. A commendable practice, but it does make it difficult to know the nature of the original setting. Certainly Jesus was acting out the corporate implications of the Son of man and the kingdom of God when he commissioned the disciples to participate in his words and works. Matthew 10:40, "He who receives you receives me, and he who receives me receives him who sent me," is also genuine. This verse expresses the representative nature of the kingdom in the same manner as the standard of judgment used in Matthew 25:40, Mark 9:37, and Luke 12:8. Once again the consistent motif of the kingdom appears in the form of personal acts of fidelity.

As for the success of the mission there remains some uncertainty, for later Jesus lamented that he would have gathered his people together as a hen gathers her brood under her wings and they would not (Matt. 23:37). Still, Luke records Jesus' jubilant response when the disciples return claiming authority over the demons: "I saw Satan fall like lightning from heaven" (Luke 10:18). The corporate activity of the reign of God in Jesus and his disciples may suffer violence (Matt. 11:12) and disappointment, but the sorrow of rejection is meliorated by the knowledge that the demonic world is being defeated (Matt. 12:28; Luke 11:20, Q).

4. After describing the experiences at Caesarea Philippi (Mark 8:31-33) and on the mount of Transfiguration (Mark 9:2-8), Mark records Jesus' remark to the sons of Zebedee that he must drink of the cup and be baptized, and so must they (Mark 10:35-40). The cup Jesus will drink is the cup of suffering, the judgment of God (Isa. 51:17; Jer. 25:15; Mark 14:36 and para.), which he drains to the dregs as the representative of men. In the two main metaphors of his ministry, the kingdom of God and the Son of man, Jesus stands forth as the representative both of God's grace and judgment, and of men's desire to overcome alienation. In him the two are incorporate, and so his activity is necessarily a ministry of sorrow as well as of joy. He must be baptized with the baptism of representative suffering for men. Luke 12:50 records the words of Jesus: "I have a baptism to be baptized with; and how I am constrained until it is accomplished!"

Whether or not Jesus anticipated death from the beginning of his ministry at the river Jordan, he understood his words and acts as the tragedy of Isaiah's suffering servant. Since John the Baptist had suffered martyrdom at an early stage of the ministry, Jesus was fully aware of the seriousness of the opposition: "From the days of John the Baptist until now the kingdom of heaven has suffered violence, and men of violence take it by force" (Matt. 11:12).

Now he turns his face toward Jerusalem, prepared to make a final expression of the kingdom in word and act, and to suffer John's fate if that is to be forced upon him. The acts of Jesus during these last days in Jerusalem are remarkably creative expressions of his faithfulness to everything he has stood for since the beginning. He begins his Jerusalem ministry with three acted parables on the order of Old Testament prophetic imagery. Jeremiah had performed many of these *ōthōth,* such as the breaking of the earthen flask to symbolize the breaking of Jerusalem (Jer. 19; cf. Jer. 27; 32; Ezek. 4; 5; Isa. 20).

Dramatized Acts

1. The first of the acted parables is the triumphant entry into the holy city (Mark 11:1-10; Matt. 21:1-9; Luke 19:28-38; cf. John 12:12-19). The demonstration that surrounded him was indeed ironic, for the people's cry, "Blessed be the kingdom of our father David that is coming," does not hail Jesus as Messiah, but voices their great eschatological expectations of national restoration. Jesus silently repudiates this patriotic dream. He had never been patriotic to begin with, at least not in the nationalistic sense, and his favorable comments on Samaritans and Gentiles had earlier brought him into trouble with the authorities. Jesus' "patriotism," if we want to call it that, was never on an external level but lay deeper in the realm of personal fidelity. Thus this acted parable is an act of peace symbolized by the beast of peace, the lowly ass. There is great irony in Zechariah 9:9, the background passage:

> Lo, your king comes to you;
> triumphant and victorious is he,

but he comes unexpectedly,

> humble and riding on an ass,
> on a colt the foal of an ass.

The kingdom of God cannot be identified with nationalism, but only with a fidelity of the heart. The second of the three acted parables bears out this motif in the cleansing of the temple (Mark 11:15-19; Matt. 21:10-17; Luke 19:45-48). Jesus had consistently opposed the hypocrisy of hollow religion: "For I tell you, unless your righteousness exceeds that of the scribes and Pharisees, you will never enter the kingdom of heaven" (Matt. 5:20). Here, in the confines of the temple itself, he renders the judgment of God upon "bad faith," for cleansing and "good faith" are tokens of the kingdom: "The

Lord whom you seek will suddenly come to his temple; . . . But who can endure the day of his coming, and who can stand when he appears? . . . he will purify the sons of Levi and refine them like gold and silver, till they present right offerings to the Lord" (Mal. 3:1-3). Perhaps the words of Zechariah 14:21*b* are even more appropriate: "And there shall no longer be a trader in the house of the Lord of hosts on that day."

In challenging those who misuse the temple and make it a place of commerce, Jesus opposes the hypocrisy of the religious authorities, but he also enacts a messianic sign of the new time. It was an expectation in Jewish tradition that the messianic age would bring a renewal of the temple, when Gentiles would worship at Mount Zion: "For my house shall be called a house of prayer for all peoples" (Isa. 56:7; cf. Ezek. 43:6 ff.). Here is one of the great corporate acts of Jesus, encompassing the whole world of men.[8] He prepares the temple for the coming in of the Gentiles, and presages the message and mission of the early Christians who discover the far-reaching implications of the kingdom: "God shows no partiality, but in every nation any one who fears him and does what is right is acceptable to him" (Acts 10:34 f.). The point is also made in Galatians 3:28-29: "There is neither Jew nor Greek, there is neither slave nor free, there is neither male nor female; for you are all one in Christ Jesus. And if you are Christ's, then you are Abraham's offspring, heirs according to promise."

The third of the acted parables is yet another corporate act of fellowship, and so important in the worship of the community that it takes on the character of a sacrament. This is the Last Supper (Mark 14:12-25; Matt. 26:17-29; Luke 22:7-19; 1 Cor. 11:23-25). The Supper was prefigured by the sacramental meal in the wilderness (Mark 6:30-44). Again there appears that symbol of the kingdom, the fellowship of the messianic banquet; and what more elemental token of fellowship than this, eating bread and drinking wine together?

Jesus had compared the kingdom of God to a fellowship meal (Luke 14:15-24; Matt. 22:1-10, Q), and now it was taking its final form in the ministry of suffering.

The cup symbolized the judgment of God which Jesus must drink for the many (Mark 10:38, 45; 14:24, 36). The sacrificial theme is certainly strong in Mark and in Paul, and though the Supper itself may have been only a preparatory meal, or kiddush, it surely took place upon the background of Passover. Perhaps it was actually a Passover meal, as the synoptics insist against the Fourth Gospel.

Yet we wonder whether the church has not accorded too great an honor to the sacrificial motif of the Supper and neglected its covenantal significance. Dom Gregory Dix may be correct when he ascribes this inordinate interest in sacrifice to the Hellenizing forces in the church, for whom the notion of a covenant-sacrifice was not so vivid as it was to the Jew.[9] Mark writes his Gospel for Gentile Christians around A.D. 65; and there we begin to detect the subtle shift from "covenant" to "blood." Paul, the Jewish Christian, uses the phrase "the new covenant in my blood," where covenant is accorded pride of place, while Mark has "this is my blood of the covenant," where the covenant is definitely subsidiary to the sacrificial idea (so also Matthew).

The unhappy result of this transformation has been the ascendancy of the sacrifice motif and the disappearance of the covenant idea in Eastern and Western versions of the mass.[10] Here is irony indeed, that a covenant meal which was essentially a *fellowship* banquet, symbolizing the unity of Jesus and his disciples (a figure of the kingdom of God), has become a divisive sacrament separating Christian from Christian.

Luke's version of the Supper is highly interesting, and it may very well be an independent unit of tradition which emphasizes the eschatological idea of the covenant. In two sayings arranged in synonymous parallelism, reminiscent of the a b, a′ b′ form of prophetic language, Jesus says:

(a) "I have earnestly desired to eat this passover with
     you before I suffer;
(b) for I tell you I shall not eat it until it is fulfilled in
     the kingdom of God" (Luke 22:15 f.).
And he took a cup, and when he had given thanks he said,
(a') "Take this, and divide it among yourselves;
(b') for I tell you that from now on I shall not drink of
     the fruit of the vine until the kingdom of God comes"
     (Luke 22:17 f.).
(Verse 19 intrudes itself upon the sense of the passage and
its literary form, and should be bracketed.)

This parallelism is a remarkable confirmation of the *communion* and *eschatological* motifs so characteristic of Jesus'
teaching in general. They are integral to the theme of the
Passover as symbolic of the fellowship of God's people, who
wait upon the fulfillment of the kingdom.

Could it not be that the original setting of the Supper was
an act of Jesus in which he characterized the nature of the
kingdom as a fellowship meal, partaken with a sense of tension
between the already and the not yet? It was meal of covenant
sacrifice, not of sacrifice alone. When we recall the corporate
nature of the other acts of Jesus, this one eminently represents
their common theme. At the meal Jesus is the representative
of his people who is about to effect a new covenant by giving
himself, and he extends to his disciples a share in this new
covenant, the kingdom soon to come in power.

2. It is quite remarkable that the conclusion of Jesus' earthly
ministry parallels its beginning. His mission is inaugurated in
an act of baptism at the river Jordan where he identifies himself with his people and experiences his filial union with the
Father. Then Jesus undergoes a testing of his fidelity in the
temptation.

In the hours of his final passion he once again withstands
a testing of his faithfulness in Gethsemane, then suffers the
baptism of death on the cross. The two extremities of his

ministry are chiasmic, a b, b' a'; and in between, his words and works are marked by the time dimensions of the kingdom —it has come, it is present, it is yet to come.

Jesus' act of filial fidelity in Gethsemane (Mark 14:32-42; Matt. 26:36-46; Luke 22:40-46) tells us something of his wholeness in the face of death. True, his prayer in the garden can only have been supplied with the aid of the witnesses' imagination, for they were dozing at some distance apart. Yet it does not seem at all possible that they later would have followed and died for one who collapsed or went to pieces in his last hours of suffering. It is unlikely that even a resurrection could have rescued their respect had he now disintegrated and repudiated everything he had stood for. *They* were guilty of bad faith, they knew that well enough, and were remorseful. But could they call him "Lord" who went to pieces at the cross, or cursed God and died?

If anything at all emerges from the analysis of Jesus' language and acts thus far, it is the note of his unitary self. This is precisely the theme of the phenomenological analysis of persons as we find it explored in Wittgenstein, Polanyi, Marcel, and others. Words cannot be separated from the person who claims them as an expression of himself. They bear his signature—intentionally—as do his acts. It simply is not possible to abstract a subject's words from his whole self, claim that they are authentic words because they disclosed existential truths, and at the same time question the good faith of the person who speaks them.

Accordingly, it would be contrary to what "person" really means were someone to say that the Christian kerygma proclaims the decisive manifestation of divine love, and then to call into question the faithfulness of Jesus in the face of his final suffering and death. The kerygma is no better than the person whose name it proclaims.

It is amazing, then, that a contemporary school of thought wants to make that very distinction. After ascribing to Jesus a prophetic consciousness, indeed a "consciousness of authority," Bultmann applies the technique of radical doubt to the final hours: It is impossible to know, he says, how Jesus understood his death, since every intimation of his final suffering is written in by the post-Easter community. There is the possibility that he saw it as a meaningless fate and, unable to bear it, suffered a collapse.[11]

Schubert Ogden assumes the same attitude. "From the critical historian's standpoint," he argues, "Jesus' death can be seen only as the result of a tragic misunderstanding of his ministry on the part of the Roman authorities. Whether he himself found any meaning in so meaningless a fate we simply do not know; indeed, the possibility that he went to pieces in facing it cannot be ruled out."[12]

Here is a remarkable statement indeed. There are two serious errors in it. First, it assumes, incorrectly, that there is such a person as *the* critical historian who can come to only one conclusion; namely, that Jesus' death was a misunderstanding. Polanyi is quite correct when he reminds us that no scholar has a standpoint of pure objectivity removed from his personal belief. There are many critical historians, some of whom do *not* conclude that because the Roman authorities misunderstood Jesus, he may therefore have suffered personal collapse. If a critical historian does personally accredit the collapse of Jesus, he cannot consistently accredit the Christian kerygma. The statement assumes that criticism somehow stands above belief—and this is unwarranted. A commitment of faith of some sort is primary in all historical interpretation. Critical doubt is secondary. It would be more accurate to speak of "fiduciary" historians, rather than "critical" historians.[13]

Second—and this is the more serious—the signal failure of the Bultmannian school is that it does not really have an adequate concept of "self." The existentialist insights of Bultmann have informed our analysis of Jesus' ministry in many instances, but his school is given to a radical disjunction between faith and a scientism, a disjunction that can no longer be sustained. As has often been noted before on these pages, the Bultmannians fail to see the integral nature of words, acts, and the person who stands in back of them.

Something is radically wrong, then, when a theologian can entertain the collapse of Jesus, yet affirm, "The entire reality of Jesus of Nazareth, including not only his preaching and acts of healing, but his fellowship with sinners and his eventual death on the cross, was transparent to the word he sought to proclaim."[14]

That last statement properly characterizes Christian belief: We *believe* Jesus was that kind of person, that his life was "transparent" to God because of his creative fidelity to the Father and to the world of men he represented. We *believe* that he was faithful, that he was a person of wholeness, to the very end. Christian faith and kerygma rest upon that belief.

3. Before Jesus and his disciples left the upper room, they would have sung Psalms 113 to 117 (supposing that they had eaten a paschal meal). The note of fidelity is strong in the words of Psalm 116:10-11, which also speak of the unfaithfulness of men:

> I kept my faith, even when I said
> "I am greatly afflicted";
> I said in my consternation,
> "Men are all a vain hope."

Certainly this servant psalm has messianic overtones and may well have been in Jesus' mind as he suffered the temptation to avoid the cross he knew he must face, but alone. The words "I kept my faith" are crucial to an understanding of the passion, because his suffering is the ultimate act of his fidelity. By contrast, the disciples prove themselves men of bad faith—Peter above all, who denies that he ever knew him (Mark 14:71 f.).

Blasphemy was the charge against Jesus before the San-
hedrin, but because a Roman procurator would understand
insurrection better than blasphemy, the charges against Jesus
in Pilate's presence were based upon his teaching of the kingdom. And so Pilate asked (Mark 15:2 and para.): "Are
you King of the Jews?" This confirms the Gospel narratives
that Jesus placed the kingdom of God foremost in his teaching, proclaiming it with such authority that the charge could
be leveled that he had said that "he himself is Christ a king"
(Luke 23:2).

Then Jesus was scourged and crucified.

How shall we interpret the cross, the final act of Jesus of
Nazareth? Miguel de Unamuno has said that "he who pities
most loves most," and that love which pierces to the innermost
"embraces all that it sees, and pities all that it embraces."[15]
In laying down his life, the life of wholeness, fidelity, love
and pity, Jesus accomplished that final act of suffering in
which he took upon himself the burden of the whole human
race. There, as the personalization of God and the corporate
representative of men, he suffered the ultimate alienation of
men from God: "My God, my God, why hast thou forsaken
me?"—and exhausted that alienation.

We cannot be sure of the exact words of Jesus from the
cross. He may have said no more than "Eloi, Eloi," "My
God, my God," the first words of Psalm 22:1. His cry cannot
in any case be taken as a cry of dereliction, for the psalm
itself is a cry of suffering in fidelity to God. The Christian
community preserved Jesus' final cry not because the members
believed it expressed his disillusionment, but because it was
the final saving act of the kingdom which he had come to fulfill. It is highly unlikely that the Christian faith would have
had the slightest following had it been common knowledge
that Jesus disintegrated in the final crucial moments of his
ministry. We can imagine the sequel if the eyewitnesses had
heard him curse God and castigate his oppressors with the

bitter imprecation of Psalm 137: "Happy shall he be who requites you with what you have done to us!"

The Christian historian believes in the consistent witness of Jesus to the very end, for the cross is the final invasion of demonic alienation by the man of incarnate wholeness, God's chosen representative. All classical theories of atonement pale before this final act of Jesus. C. H. Dodd has caught perhaps better than any other the meaning of this corporate act of at-one-ment:

(1) The Servant incorporates in himself the whole people of God; his death therefore is their death; his resurrection their resurrection. His death therefore is vicarious, or more properly representative. (2) As such it is an "offering for sin." It expiates sin by exhausting its consequences.[16]

"By exhausting its consequences"— that is it exactly. The cross is the supreme act of a life that exhausts the threat of a bedeviled, fragmented world and calls attention to the suffering of God who "so loved the world that he gave his only Son." Is it possible on principle that a human life could manifest the wholeness of God in fidelity to the very end? That is what Jesus demanded of men—complete, creative fidelity, *and* it is what the Christian kerygma proclaims Jesus accomplished as the very personalization of God's wholeness.

4. In Jesus of Nazareth, God made a creative passage of tremendous significance to the world. In the total "event" of the life of Jesus, God added something once for all. Upon this consummate life of wholeness he set his seal of approval— the resurrection—and raised Jesus of Nazareth to cosmic significance for every man. In the resurrection, Jesus rose into the kerygma, and rises again wherever he is proclaimed, enabling men to rise out of lostness to the wholeness of God. The resurrection gives rise to the kerygma, and the kerygma makes the completeness of Jesus an existential possibility for every man in every moment.

But this possibility does not exhaust the meaning of the resurrection, for it has its equally important past and future dimensions. Rising to newness of life in the present is possible only because God placed his imprimatur upon the life Jesus lived: He demonstrated in the resurrection of Jesus that neither the demonic hypocrisy and blindness of men nor the final threat of death can overcome that kind of life. The resurrection is the completion of the passion, concluding upon a note of triumph and exhausting every threat of alienation and nihilism.

The resurrection *happened*. The fiduciary historian who trusts in the first witnesses to this momentous act of God believes that he raised Jesus from the dead. The Christian historian may question the fragmentary details of the empty tomb, but he affirms with the apostle Paul that Christian faith begins with our trust in the proclamation that Jesus of Nazareth was raised to a new dimension of personal existence (1 Cor. 15:1-7, 12-20), and that he is the "firstfruits" of the resurrection every believer may anticipate. Paul struggles to describe this metamorphosis of the self. He uses the analogy of the seed that is sown and that fructifies into something continuous yet wonderfully discontinuous with what is sown. He draws upon the metaphors of nature to illustrate that resurrection is a fact in the lower kingdom; it is also a fact in the personal kingdom because of what God has accomplished in Jesus the Messiah. Paul describes the resurrection body as a *sōma pneumatikon,* a spiritual body (1 Cor. 15:44); it exists within a dimension related to yet different from our own, for "flesh and blood cannot inherit the kingdom of God" (1 Cor. 15:50).

A problem arises in connection with the various descriptions of the risen Jesus in the Gospel narratives, some of which appear to be contradictory. For example, according to the Lucan account of his appearance in Jerusalem (Luke 24:36-43), the risen Jesus points to his flesh and bones and eats a piece of broiled fish. We detect in this and in the often beautifully detailed accounts of the empty tomb a later tendency in the tradition to materialize the resurrection.

However, these imaginative embroideries of faith must not detract attention from the universal agreement of the witnesses that Jesus *had risen*. The earliest witnesses do not speak of the reanimation of the corpse but, like Paul, write of the continuation of the person Jesus in a new dimension of personal existence.

The skeptical interpreter may elect to believe in the illusion of immortality, but for the early Christians, as for later Christians, the good news of the gospel is that the future certainty of death holds no terror of personal annihilation, but is a transition to a new dimension of the inexhaustible multidimensionality of the kingdom of God. The hope of future resurrection releases us from anxiety toward the future, and gives us back our present where we are free to live in creative fidelity. Jesus' eschatological teaching has exactly this same effect of releasing the believer from fear of the future so that he may live creatively in the present.

So tremendous is this good news that Paul can only describe it as *dynamis,* power. The cross, he writes, is the *dynamis* of God (1 Cor. 1:18, 24); in the resurrection Jesus is designated Son of God in power (*en dynamei*) (Rom. 1:4); Christ "is not weak in dealing with you, but is powerful (*dynatei*) in you. For he was crucified in weakness, but lives by the power (*ek dynameōs*) of God" (2 Cor. 13:3 f.); "And God raised the Lord and will also raise us up by his power (*dia tēs dynameōs autou*)" (1 Cor. 6:14; 15:43).

An element of mystery surrounds the resurrection. But mystery is the matrix of all knowing. The witnesses to Jesus' resurrection do not claim to understand the mystery of God's doing, but they do proclaim a momentous act of God which changed their lives, and can change the life of every man. The Christian believes their witness, and in that believing discovers a present and a future open to the freedom and creativity that was forgotten of men until God came in Jesus Christ to awaken them out of forgetfulness.

READINGS ON CHAPTER FIVE

Beare, Francis W. *The Earliest Records of Jesus.* New York. Abingdon Press, 1962.

Braaten, Carl E., and Harrisville, Roy A. (eds. and trans.). *The Historical Jesus and the Kerygmatic Christ: Essays on the New Quest of the Historical Jesus.* New York: Abingdon Press, 1964.

Dix, Dom Gregory. *Jew and Greek.* New York: Harper & Row, n.d.

Dodd, C. H. *According to the Scriptures.* London: Nisbet & Co., 1953.

Grant, Robert M. *A Historical Introduction to the New Testament.* New York: Harper & Row, 1963.

Hartshorne, Charles. *The Logic of Perfection and Other Essays in Neoclassical Metaphysics.* La Salle, Ill.: Open Court Publishing Co., 1962.

Hennecke, Edgar. *New Testament Apocrypha,* Vol. I, ed. Wilhelm Schneemelcher. Translated by R. McL. Wilson. Philadelphia: Westminster Press, 1963.

Hume, David. *An Enquiry Concerning Human Understanding. (Philosophic Classics, Bacon to Kant,* ed. Walter Kaufmann.) Englewood Cliffs, N. J.: Prentice-Hall, 1961.

Jeremias, Joachim. *Jesus' Promise to the Nations.* Translated by S. H. Hooke. ("Studies in Biblical Theology," No. 24.) London: SCM Press, 1958.

Käsemann, Ernst. *Essays on New Testament Themes.* Translated by W. J. Montague. ("Studies in Biblical Theology," No. 41.) London: SCM Press, 1964.

Marcel, Gabriel. *Creative Fidelity.* Translated by Robert Rosthal. New York: Noonday Press, 1964.

Niebuhr, Richard R. *Resurrection and Historical Reason.* New York: Charles Scribner's Sons, 1957.

Ogden, Schubert M. *Christ Without Myth: A Study Based on the Theology of Rudolph Bultmann.* New York: Harper & Row, 1961.

Polanyi, Michael. *Personal Knowledge: Towards a Post-Critical Philosophy*. Harper Torchbooks; New York: Harper & Row, 1964.

Unamuno, Miguel de. *The Tragic Sense of Life*. Translated by J. E. C. Flitch. New York: Dover, 1954.

Whitehead, Alfred North. *Adventures of Ideas*. New York: Macmillan, 1948.

PART II

CHRIST, EXISTENCE,

AND THE

KINGDOM OF GOD

CHAPTER SIX

The
Kingdom of God
and the
Christ of Faith

WHEN JESUS was raised from the dead by the power of God, he was raised to cosmic significance. He rose into the kerygma. His followers could only proclaim with enthusiasm what they had seen and heard. A great joy overwhelmed them when they discovered that the enemy—death—had been overcome by the sacrifice of his life and in the divine power of the resurrection.

Now they enthusiastically preached a message of newness of life which centered upon the person through whom God had acted to reveal to men the mystery of existence.

But for some strange reason, the metaphors of the kingdom of God and the Son of man, which had been so much a part of Jesus' language, practically dropped out of use in the early church except for scattered appearances. The book of Acts mentions the kingdom on only eight occasions—surprising, for we should have expected to find it figuring importantly in the preaching of the early community, when Jesus had so often proclaimed its coming. Paul's great theological document to the Roman church mentions it but once, so also 1 and 2 Thessalonians, Galatians, Ephesians, James, and 2 Peter. It appears as seldom in other New Testament sources: twice each in Colossians, 2 Timothy, and Hebrews, and five times in both 1 Corinthians and Revelation. The Son of man teaching disappears entirely except for one lonely reference in Acts 7:56.

Why? we ask. Several answers have been suggested. For one, in the Gentile mission the Jewish notion of a divine reign was simply not a relevant metaphor through which to introduce the gospel. No message to the Gentiles would extol a Jewish king. Another plausible suggestion is that the preaching of the kingdom could have led the church into unnecessary difficulties with the Roman authorities. Was not Jesus himself crucified on suspicion of insurrection because it was reported that he had preached on the theme of kingship?

Both suggestions are well taken, yet was the Christian community all that pragmatic? If it were trouble they were avoiding, they never stopped proclaiming Christ crucified and risen, and that persistence cost many of them their lives. As for the irrelevance of the kingdom idea to Gentiles, Paul complained that the crucifixion was as much foolishness to the Gentiles as it was a stumbling block to the Jews (1 Cor. 1:23), yet he never gave up proclaiming the cross. Besides, when the Gospels were written there was a considerable Gentile mission and a constant threat of persecution from the state, yet the Evangelists never hesitated to record Jesus' continual use of the kingdom metaphor. These Gospels, Mark and Luke at least, were designed for predominantly Gentile communities, and there was always the likelihood that some of these copies would fall into the hands of Roman authorities.

We are not above allowing that the early church was flexible and pragmatic in adapting the kerygma to new situations. Far from it, for we shall have to explain Paul's de-emphasis of Christ from a human point of view (2 Cor. 5:16) as his reaction to a contextual problem at Corinth where certain competitors were overemphasizing Jesus as a kind of "divine man." In that context he chose to play down the role of the historical Jesus. Christian interpreters could adapt themselves to many situations, there is no question about that.

But there must have been a more convincing reason why the earliest Christians saw fit virtually to strike the kingdom motif from their own vocabulary. The answer is that after the resurrection experience, the disciples realized that Jesus had all the while been talking about a spiritual reign embodied in himself. They awakened to the fact that he had refashioned the kingdom of God into something unimaginably greater than it had been before, and that he had no intention of restoring the politically oriented Davidic kingdom to Israel (an idea that persisted among his followers even after the resurrection; see Acts 1:6). Accordingly, they turned from the concept of the kingdom to the person who personalized the kingdom, weaving their theology about him. Outside the Gospels, the person of Jesus Christ displaces the abstract terminology of the Son of man and the kingdom of God. It is he who is proclaimed, not the kingdom. P. T. Forsyth was straight on the mark when he wrote:

The King is the Kingdom. To be "in Christ" is to be in the Kingdom. . . . The apostolic preaching of Christ therefore took the place of Christ's own preaching of the Kingdom. . . . The Gospel of the Kingdom was Christ in essence; Christ was the Gospel of the Kingdom in power. The Kingdom was Christ in a mystery; Christ was the publication, the establishment of the Kingdom. To bring the Kingdom preach the King. He was the truth of his own greatest Gospel. It is wherever he is. To have him is to ensure it.[1]

The Kerygma of the Earliest Christians: Christ Is the Kingdom

To be "in Christ" is to be in the kingdom: That is the key to the apostolic witness. The belief that Jesus is the Messiah gave rise to the kerygma of the early church, and it is the theme that unifies the diversity of the New Testament. It proceeds from the original kerygma found in the opening words of Jesus' ministry: "The time has come; the kingdom of God is upon you; repent, and believe the Gospel" (Mark 1:15, NEB). In the two main sources of the apostolic kerygma (the Acts speeches and the earliest traditions in Paul's writings), the good news is proclaimed in full view of Jesus' person. The three points of Jesus' kerygma are:

(a) The time has come (or is fulfilled);
(b) the kingdom of God is upon you;
(c) repent, and believe the gospel.

These become in view of the whole ministry of Jesus:

(a') The prophecies are fulfilled, the new age of God has begun (Acts 2:16; 10:43; Rom. 1:2; 1 Cor. 15:3 f.).

(b') The long-awaited Messiah, born of David's line, has come (Acts 2:30 f.; 13:22 f.; Rom. 1:3). He is Jesus of Nazareth, who, after John's baptism, did mighty works by the power of God (Acts 10:37 f.), died on a tree for our sins (Acts 5:30; 10:39; Gal. 3:13), has been raised from the dead by the power of God (Acts 2:24, 32; 3:15), and is exalted to God's right hand (Acts 2:33; Rom. 8:34), and will come again as judge and savior (Acts 3:20 f.; 10:42; Rom. 2:16; 1 Thess. 1:10).

(c') Therefore repent, and be baptized for the forgiveness of your sins (Acts 2:38; 3:19; 10:43).

The first and third sections of both proclamations are practically identical. In Jesus' announcement and in the preaching of the early church, (a) the time is now fulfilled, and (c) all hearers are exhorted to repent and believe. But what has happened to the second section? Precisely this. Where Jesus proclaimed the arrival of the kingdom of God, the apostles now herald the life, the death and exaltation of Jesus himself. The earliest preaching of the church interprets Jesus as the living fulfillment of the kingdom of God. For them, membership in the kingdom is nothing else than being "in Christ" through faith. To proclaim the kingdom is to proclaim a completed life in whom the redeeming rule of God came and comes and will come to all who believe. Thus the second section of the kerygma proclaims not only the past event of redemption (works, death, resurrection) but also the present exaltation of Christ which is his work of intercession for men (cf. Rom. 8:34), and the Parousia when Christ will consummate the kingdom as savior and judge (cf. Acts 3:20 f.; 10:42). The apostolic kerygma expresses an eschatology that is existentially relevant because the wholeness of Jesus Christ is proclaimed to be the Way for every man (Acts 10:43; 24:22).

The Pauline Tradition: The Kingdom Is Life in Christ

Most of the references to the kingdom of God in the Pauline material are warnings and exhortations that only the pure can inherit the kingdom: "The kingdom of God does not consist in talk but in power" (1 Cor. 4:20); it "does not mean food and drink but righteousness and peace and joy in the Holy Spirit" (Rom. 14:17). Immorality has no place in the kingdom, for only the righteous partake of its blessings (1 Cor. 6:9 f.; 15:50; Gal. 5:21; Eph. 5:5; 1 Thess. 2:12). In light of the kingdom, all else appears to be of the dominion of darkness from which God has delivered us (Col. 1:13). We are to be made worthy of the kingdom through suffering, in which we are exhorted to continue without flinching or complaining (2 Thess. 1:5; 2 Tim. 4:1, 5). The relationship of suffering and the kingdom recalls Jesus' words about sharing his suffering and drinking his cup (Mark 10:39); the exhortation to be pure and whole is, of course, crucial to his ministry.

In Acts 28:23 and 31, Luke summarizes the ministry of Paul at Rome by placing Christ and the kingdom in apposition: "And he expounded the matter to them from morning till evening, testifying to the kingdom of God and trying to convince them about Jesus both from the law of Moses and from the prophets . . . , preaching the kingdom of God and teaching about the Lord Jesus Christ." It is certainly right to read the two interchangeably. Indeed, this is exactly what Paul did himself when he worked out the implications of the gospel. It came to a single theme: *life in Christ*.

1. Life in Christ is a Personal Relationship.

Paul's idea of the kingdom as life in Christ can be put in the mystical words of Galatians 2:20: "I have been crucified with Christ; it is no longer I who live, but Christ who lives in me; and the life I now live in the flesh I live by faith in the Son of God, who loved me and gave himself for me." As James Denney once expressed it in a memorable passage:

Christ is the whole of Christianity—Christ crucified and risen. He is the whole of it on the external side, regarded as the revelation and action of God for the salvation of sinful men; and faith in Christ—that abandonment of the soul to Him in which Paul as a Christian lived and moved and had his being—is the whole of it on the internal side. . . . His faith in Christ was such that it admitted of no other object; Christ completely filled his religious horizon; his whole being, as a spiritual man with a life toward God, depended upon and was determined by Christ alone.[2]

Yet Paul was only following another when he equated "life" with the kingdom of God; Jesus himself had made the equation. For in Mark 9:43, 45 we find Jesus saying:

"It is better for you to enter *life* maimed than with two hands to go to hell."

"It is better for you to enter *life* lame than with two feet to be thrown into hell."

And then in Mark 9:47:

"It is better for you to enter *the kingdom of God* with one eye than with two eyes to be thrown into hell."

The words are interchangeable. Again, the question of the rich young ruler, "What must I do to inherit eternal life?"

(Mark 10:17), is paralleled by Jesus' comment to his disciples in Mark 10:23: "How hard it will be for those who have riches to enter *the kingdom* of God!" The young man wanted eternal life, but he failed the test because he valued his possessions too highly. Jesus then implies that his riches are keeping him out of the kingdom of God and from obtaining eternal life. Eternal life and the kingdom of God are one and the same in Jesus' understanding (cf. Mark 10:30 where mention of eternal life follows upon the discussion of the kingdom, and Luke 18:29 f. where the two are placed in apposition). Again, Jesus parallels the saying "Enter by the narrow gate . . . ; For the gate is narrow and the way is hard, that leads to life, and those who find it are few" (Matt. 7:13 f.) with "Not every one who says to me, 'Lord, Lord,' shall enter the kingdom of heaven, but he who does the will of my Father who is in heaven" (Matt. 7:21). Both life and the kingdom can be entered because they are synonymous. At the Last Judgment the king says to the righteous on his right hand, "Come, O blessed of my Father, inherit the kingdom prepared for you" (Matt. 25:34), and shortly after he says that they are to go into eternal life (Matt. 25:46).

"Life," then, *is* the kingdom for Paul as it is for Jesus, and being "in Christ" is that life. Accordingly, in Paul's gospel Christ is the kingdom, and he nearly exhausts his vocabulary describing the felicity of living in him and with him: "For the kingdom of God . . . [is] righteousness and peace and joy in the Holy Spirit; he who thus serves Christ is acceptable to God and approved by men" (Rom. 14:17 f.). As here, so elsewhere Paul often uses Christ and the Holy Spirit interchangeably. For instance, Paul interchanges "the Spirit is in you," "Christ is in you," "the Spirit of Christ is in you" (Rom. 8:9-11), and, similarly, the Spirit intercedes for us (Rom. 8:26 f.) as does the Son (Rom. 8:34). In the Gospel According to John as well, Jesus refers to himself indirectly as a paraclete or counselor: "And I will pray the Father, and he will give you another Counselor; . . . you know him, for he dwells with you, and will be in you" (John 14:16 f.). As the Spirit was with the disciples in Jesus during his ministry, so now Christ is with us in the Spirit (cf. also 1 John 2:1 where Christ is spoken of as an advocate). So interpreted, Romans 14:17 f. further evidences Paul's equation of Christ and the kingdom of God.

Paul goes on to develop the idea of life in Christ some two hundred times (including the expressions "in the Lord" and "in him"), tying this mystical concept to every noble quality that lies at hand—it is being washed, sanctified, and justified "in the name of the Lord Jesus Christ and in the Spirit of our God" (1 Cor. 6:11); it is becoming "the righteousness of God" (2 Cor. 5:21); it is becoming sons of God "through faith" (Gal. 3:26) and being "all one in Christ Jesus" (Gal. 3:28); it is the free gift of God and eternal life "in Christ Jesus our Lord" (Rom. 6:23); it is rejoicing (Phil. 3:1; Rom. 14:17); it is "the peace of God, which passes all understanding," which "will keep your hearts and your minds in Christ Jesus" (Phil. 4:7); it is being sealed (Eph. 1:13, 4:30) and "circumcised with a circumcision made without hands, by putting off the body of flesh in the circumcision of Christ" (Col. 2:11); it is being filled (Eph. 5:18). It also affects our language, for "as men of sincerity, as commissioned by God, in the sight of God we speak in Christ" (2 Cor. 2:17; cf. 1 Cor. 12:3; Rom. 9:1; Eph. 4:15). In a word, "life in Christ" is the wholeness of the kingdom which Jesus brought to realization in his life. He was the man of sincerity, commissioned by God, who spoke in the sight of God; and because of his wholeness we also may become whole. Paul sees this as an eschatology of process: "Our inner nature is *being renewed (anakainoutai)* every day" (2 Cor. 4:16), "we all . . . are *being changed (metamorphoumetha)* into his likeness from one degree of glory to another" (2 Cor. 3:18) *"until* Christ be formed" in us (Gal. 4:19). The metamorphosis is

144

existential: it works itself out in the process of the present, yet stands ahead of itself (*ex-istere*) into the "until" of the future.

2. Life in Christ is a Societary Relationship.

But life in Christ does not end with inward experience; his disciples do not hide their light under a bushel once they have come to know him. Life in Christ is the fellowship of a community of believers. Like the kingdom of God and the Son of man, life in Christ is a fundamentally corporate experience.

What evidence do we own for this societary interpretation? First, Jesus Christ is the second Adam who has brought a reign of life where there had been a reign of death: "If, because of one man's trespass, death reigned through that one man, much more will those who receive the abundance of grace and the free gift of righteousness reign in life through the one man Jesus Christ" (Rom. 5:17; cf. 1 Cor. 15:22). Next, in an important metaphor Paul compares us to a body: "So we, though many, are one body in Christ, and individually members one of another" (Rom. 12:5; cf. 1 Cor. 10:17; 12:12 ff.; Eph. 4:25). Again, Paul likens us to sons of God who have "put on Christ" through faith. There are no differences between Jew and Gentile, slaves or free, male or female in the kingdom of God, "For you are all one in Christ Jesus" (Gal. 3:28; Rom. 10:12). The cross which has brought us all together was necessary, says Paul, "that in Christ Jesus the blessings of Abraham might come upon the Gentiles, that we might receive the promise of the Spirit through faith" (Gal. 3:14). The societary nature of life in Christ confirms the phenomenological analysis of existence which views reality as fundamentally social (thus Whitehead and Hartshorne).

3. Life in Christ is a Relationship of Love.

What is the vital force that holds the body of men together? Paul finds the answer in agape, the deepest and most inclusive kind of love. Above all, he says, "put on love, which binds everything together in perfect harmony" (Col. 3:14), for without love "I am nothing" (*outhen eimi,* 1 Cor. 13:2 f.). A subject lives inauthentically if he does not love. To be is to be together, *esse est co-esse,* a truth which emerges from the acts and language of Jesus; and that which holds men together is love. Hence the "I" that does not love is nothing, since the "I" comes into being only in relationship with others. Here again, the implication is that the subject becomes an authentic person only if he is committed to his words and acts in the community of persons—and committed in love. Otherwise he is merely playing a role of mere gestures. It is like the empty role that leads to the demonic alienation called "legion."

Love possesses the attributes of societary relationship. It is patient and kind, not jealous or boastful, arrogant or rude; does not insist on its own way; is not irritable or resentful; does not rejoice at wrong, but rejoices in the right. "Love bears all things, believes all things, hopes all things, endures all things" (1 Cor. 13:7). Of faith, hope, and love, these three, "the greatest of these is love" (1 Cor. 13:13).

Accordingly, the Pauline understanding of Jesus' mission as the Christ is that men grow together in agape as an integral body; they are to aspire to become like God who loves all creatures without envy or malice, who loves them with an infinite capacity to enter into their weal and woe, hence to "relativize himself."[3] One of the truly great Pauline passages which combines nearly everything that needs to be said about the sociality of reality, the integrity of language and act, the process of God, the vitality of love, and the centrality of Christ, is Ephesians 4:15-16: "Rather, speaking the truth in love, we are to grow up in every way into him who is the head, into Christ, from whom the whole body, joined and knit together by every joint with which it is supplied, when each part is working properly, makes bodily growth and upbuilds itself in love."

It is one of those incredible inspirations of Paul which leaves us breathless before its comprehensive scope. It says everything that needs to be said of existence. It is a truly primordial utterance.

That Paul speaks for the early church, and more, that he proclaims the very gospel of love Jesus proclaimed, is clear enough. Paul's societary community knit together by love is a continuation of the central thread of Jesus' ministry. There is no difference between life in the kingdom and life in Christ. What we do have in Paul is a profound exploration of Jesus' kerygma, a cosmic expansion of Jesus' personalization of love and wholeness. When men live in the divine love, they are in Christ, in the kingdom of God, in the Son of man.

Are they justified, then, who distinguish agape from ordinary human love, eros, as Anders Nygren has done?[4] Yes, when the point is made that eros is cautious and overly self-interested, while agape is not prudentially motivated but open and uncalculating. No, where there is an inclination to mark an absolute disjunction between the two. It cannot be maintained that agape is wholly selfless and that eros is totally selfish, for a love that finds no fulfillment in loving is no love at all. Love is the desire for sociality, and that means that there is a receiving as well as a giving in every loving relationship. God himself not only gives in love but finds joy in love which is returned. Though it is possible for Platonic eros to be extended indefinitely through universal desire, agape is distinguished by its purity: it loves the unlovely as well as the lovely, hence is free of the hubris, or contempt, which affects human forms of loving. The difference between agape and eros lies in the purity and scope of their sociality.

Human forms of love bear the mark of a kind of wholeness: sensual love is love between two individuals, and no one else may enter the circle. But it is a beautiful love, and who will deny it? The members of a family love one another with a family love (*storgē*) that forbids intimacy to others. Yet who will fault it? The love of friends, philia, is a larger circle still, though it excludes most of the larger world. But will anyone say a word against it, or call it demonic? Does not the gospel itself come to us through the ordinary models of love we experience as children, parents, lovers, friends? Are not all of them metaphors that the gospel heightens to introduce us to the whole and expansive love of God? There is no absolute contrast between eros and agape, but there is an absolute separation between agape and hubris. The issue is joined where compassion confronts contempt.

Jesus uses the simple parable of a man who loves to lead us to the love of the Father. Paul employs the love of a person, Jesus Christ, to deepen our sensitivity to the purity of divine love. The difference between agape and eros is not that one is sacred and the other profane, but that agape compassionately encompasses the universe in all its dimensions. The kerygma of Jesus and of Paul assumes that men know something of love and, finding in that knowledge a common ground where God already manifests himself, proclaims the inexhaustible wholeness and universality of divine love. As God loves, so are we to love and grow up in every way, upbuilding in love the world which is the body of God.

4. Life in Christ is a Relationship of the Future as well as the Present.

Jesus' language of the kingdom is full of expectation, for the future also belongs to God. This belief releases man to be truly creative in the present. The tension between the now and the not yet disperses dread and fills him instead with creative anxiety, which is the exhilarating sense of personal meaning.

Paul's understanding of Christian existence is parallel to Jesus' own. For him the future dimension of time is inextricably tied to the past historical event of Jesus and the present historic power of Christ. We are working for a future that belongs to God, and as he has acted in the past and is present with us now, so will he act in the future (2 Thess. 1:10, 12; 2 Cor. 5:1 ff.). Did Paul expect the return of Christ and the fulfillment of all things in his own lifetime? Very likely, though his later writings are not any clearer about the time than the eschatological sayings of Jesus. What is important for Paul, as it is for Jesus, is his understanding of time: there is a future, and it belongs to God. Death itself holds no dread (Phil. 3:21). The believer is released to the present to upbuild himself and the community in love. The prodigious activity of Paul witnesses to the power of this belief in his own life. Jesus manifests the same prodigious creativity with his gospel of the kingdom.

The Johannine Writings: The Kingdom Is Eternal Life

In the scriptural writings of John, Jesus' teaching of the kingdom of God is translated into the concept of eternal life and identified with Christ in much the same way as it is in Paul. John's Gospel is written with the cosmic significance of Jesus Christ well in the foreground; for that reason the Fourth Gospel has figured only occasionally in this study of Jesus' ministry. That does not mean that there is not valuable historical material in the Gospel which sheds light on Jesus' language, acts, and intention, as C. D. Dodd has recently shown,[5] but it is clear that John was interested in viewing Jesus preeminently as the cosmic Christ. John writes, accordingly, from his inspired impressions of the incarnate Logos. The fact that in his Gospel the kingdom of God teaching is virtually replaced by the theme of eternal life reveals the flexibility of the community as it seeks to express the divine dimensions of Christ.

We must now compare the kerygma of John and Paul, gathering the evidence to show that they share much the same understanding of Jesus Christ. Employing the same pattern used in studying Paul, we shall look at John's translation of the kingdom in terms of the person of Christ.

1. The kingdom of God is eternal life. In Jesus' conversation with Nicodemus, the Fourth Evangelist selects the theme of his Gospel. To this ruler of the Jews Jesus says, "Unless one is born anew, he cannot see the kingdom of God; . . . unless one is born of water and the Spirit, he cannot enter the kingdom of God" (John 3:3, 5). What does Jesus mean by "seeing" and "entering" the kingdom of God? Simply this, as he explains shortly after: "As Moses lifted up the serpent in the wilderness, so must the Son of man be lifted up, that whoever believes in him may have *eternal life*" (John 3:14 f.). There follows the important saying in John 3:16 which joins rebirth and entering the kingdom (John 3:3, 5) with eternal life and belief in the Son. All are equated. At the end of the discourse (which is interrupted by John 3:22-30), Jesus sums up his teaching with an identical thought: "He who believes in the Son has eternal life; he who does not obey the Son shall not see life, but the wrath of God rests upon him" (John 3:36). Hence, to see life is to see the kingdom, to be reborn to new life is to enter the kingdom. To see life is to see the Son. To see the Son is to see the kingdom. So in the Fourth Gospel "to inherit eternal life" and "to enter into the kingdom of God" are interchangeable terms.

While the kingdom of God metaphor appears only twice in the Gospel and not at all in the Epistles of John, the words "life" and "eternal life" crop up in both with splendid regularity. In the Gospel the words occur no less than thirty-six times, and in 1 John thirteen times. John's use of eternal life closely resembles Paul's "life in Christ" theme and the apostolic kerygma, both of which emphasize the person and ministry of Christ rather than the kingdom of God.

2. Eternal life is Jesus Christ himself. All through John's writings there is a consistent equation of Christ and life, and the reader is left in no doubt about John's impression.

Already in John's third chapter, there are hints of the relationship. In a series of metaphors that seem to explode one after another, Jesus compares himself to:

a. Water which is life-giving (John 4:7-26). To the woman of Samaria Jesus implies that he is the true water of life, in contrast to the material water of the well: "The water that I shall give him will become in him a spring of water welling up to eternal life" (John 4:14). This utterance allows Jesus to end his discussion with the woman on the note of messiahship: "I who speak to you am he" (John 4:26), which is the same as if he had said, "I am the true water—the Christ— who will give you eternal life" (cf. Jer. 2:13 where the Lord calls himself the fountain of living waters). Later Jesus proclaims, "If any one thirst, let him come to me and drink. He who believes in me, as the scripture has said, 'Out of his heart shall flow rivers of living water' " (John 7:37 f.). It is hard to imagine language more elemental than this.

b. Bread which is life-giving (John 6). The sacramental feeding of the multitude creates the proper atmosphere for Jesus' words about bread and eternal life. It is a token of the truth that in Jesus the blessings of the kingdom are now realized. But the people misunderstand his intentions and try to make him a political king by force (John 6:15), not realizing that it is Jesus who must take them by force—by faith—"Do not labor for the food which perishes, but for the food which endures to eternal life, which the Son of man will give to you" (John 6:27). What is this bread which comes down from heaven and gives life to the world, they want to know, eager to have it always (John 6:33 f.). Jesus replies: *"I am the bread of life;* he who comes to me shall not hunger, and he who believes in me shall never thirst" (John 6:35). The identification is complete and unmistakable. But still they do not understand; he has to repeat it again and again. It is the will of the Father "that every one who sees the Son and believes in him should have eternal life" (John 6:40), for "I,

[Jesus] am the living bread which came down from heaven; if any one eats of this bread, he will live for ever" (John 6:51). Then significantly Jesus, as the one who brings eternal life, unites his mission with the passion, for whoever eats his flesh and drinks his blood has eternal life (John 6:53-58; cf. 10:11, 15, 18). It is Jesus' death which is to make life available to men, that they may dwell in him and he in them. The words of this section are inescapably eucharistic, for John has in mind the significance of the cup and the bread personified in the life given for men, that in this life they might live eternally.

c. Light which is life-giving. "I am the light of the world; he who follows me will not walk in darkness, but will have the light of life" (John 8:12). These are the words that open chapter 8 and continue in chapter 9 with the healing of the man born blind. The healing is an acted parable that accredits his words, "I came into this world, that those who do not see may see" (John 9:39). According to the synoptics, it is a light which men share in him, for they too become "the light of the world" (Matt. 5:14), but only so long as they abide in him (Luke 6:39; Matt. 15:14, Q).

d. The good shepherd who is life-giving. The thief comes only to steal, kill, and destroy, but Jesus is the door and the good shepherd who has come that they may have life, and have it abundantly (John 10:10). As the door (John 10:1 ff., 7) Jesus is "the way, and the truth, and the life," and there is no entrance to the Father but by him (John 14:6). The life which the sheep are to receive is the life of the shepherd himself who lays down everything for his sheep (John 10:11, 15). Jesus *is* that life—"he is the expiation for our sins" (1 John 2:2; 4:9 f.). In the next chapter the metaphor of the shepherd and the sheep will deserve more attention as a pointer to the intimate relationship which exists between Christ and the community of men.

e. The resurrection which is life. In a remarkable saying

152

(John 11:25 f.) Jesus calls himself the resurrection as well as the life, and says that whoever believes in him, "though he die, yet shall he live"—indeed, in a very real sense he shall never die. Why? Because the kingdom of God—eternal life —has already come in Christ, and to have him is to have the blessings of eternity in the present. This is realized eschatology—"he who hears my word and believes him who sent me, *has* eternal life; he does not come into judgment, but has passed from death to life" (John 5:24).

In these metaphors, then, Jesus equates himself with eternal life in a manner which is well summarized in 1 John 5:11 f.: "God gave us eternal life, and this life is in his Son. He who has the Son has life; he who has not the Son of God has not life. . . ." "And we are in him who is true, in his Son Jesus Christ. This is the true God and eternal life" (1 John 5:20). Accordingly, for John eternal life is the same as the kingdom of God; Jesus is the kingdom.

3. Eternal life is a personal and a communal relationship. As with Paul, so for John the life of the believer is not only personal but also societary. To believe is first a matter of personal decision, as witness Jesus' concern for Nicodemus, the woman of Samaria, the paralyzed man at Bethzatha, the man born blind, Lazarus and his sisters—all of whom he loved as persons, as he loves all men. Moreover, eternal life is a continual personal experience of coming to know Christ better: "And this is eternal life, that they *know* thee (*ginōskosin*) the only true God, and Jesus Christ whom thou hast sent" (John 17:3). So also in John 10:38: "that you may *know* (*gnōte,* ingressive aorist) and understand (*ginōskēte,* progressive present) that the Father is in me and I am in the Father."

Yet once the initial step toward redemption has been taken in faith, the believer's experience becomes communal as well, for as John 1:12 records: "All who received him, who believed in his name, he gave power to become *children* of

God." The sacramental meal in the wilderness was a communal fellowship that foreshadowed the Last Supper (John 6). We are the *sheep*, Jesus is the Shepherd (John 10); he loved to the end *his own* who were in the world (John 13:1); the servants are to do to one another as the master has done to them at the foot washing (John 13:15); in the Father's mansion there are many rooms (John 14:2 f.), a figure that symbolizes the corporate life of the family. Similar to the metaphor of the shepherd and the sheep is the symbol of the vine and its branches (John 15:1-8); in fact, the intimate relationship to Christ and to one another is even clearer in the second metaphor than in the first, for here we are living parts of the vine, integrally and inseparably related to Christ and to every other branch. Again, he calls us friends (John 15:15), and has made us sharers in his sufferings (John 15:20). In his high-priestly prayer (John 17) Jesus says he has manifested himself to the body of men whom the Father has given him (John 17:6). We note the frequency of the corporate words "they" and "them" in the chapter: "I am praying," he says, "for those whom thou hast given me, for they are thine; all mine are thine, and thine are mine, and I am glorified in them" (John 17:9 f.). Here again is that mystical relationship between the Father, the Son, and the community (cf. John 14:20), wherein they participate in Christ's glory while he is glorified in them.

Jesus then prays the Father that the members of the community may be one, even as the Father and Son are one, adding that he has kept, guarded, and sanctified them in his name (John 17:11 f.). Then he prays for those who will be brought to him through the preaching of the community, that they too may be one (John 17:20-23). Hence Jesus' high-priestly prayer includes the community's fellowship with him and the members' fellowship with one another, and it points the members to the outward proclamation of the gospel that the community of believers may grow. In 1 John 1:2 f., the apostle writes of "the eternal life which . . . was made manifest to us . . . so that you may have *fellowship* with us; and our fellowship is with the Father and with his Son Jesus Christ." Fellowship in Christ is the theme of this letter, whose author is concerned to bring all men into harmony with Christ: "If we walk in the light, as he is in the light," he says, "we have fellowship with one another" (1 John 1:7), and we can then be said to be "in him," "with him," "of him" (1 John 1:3; 2:5 f., 8, 27 f.; 3:5 f., 24; 4:2, 4, 6, 9, 13, 15 f.; 5:14, 18-20), just as he is said to be equally "in us" (1 John 2:5, 8, 23, 27; 3:24; 4:4, 12 f., 15 f.; 5:10, 12). We are God's children, part of his family (1 John 3:1 f., 10; 5:1 f.; cf. John 1:12). Finally, the community spirit is apparent in the word brethren, with which John links a vital word in the fellowship of believers—love: "We know that we have passed out of death into life, because we love the brethren" (1 John 3:14).

4. Eternal life is a relationship of love. As with Paul, eternal love is the highest type of love for John, except that the latter makes no distinction between *phileō* and *agapaō*. The mark of passing into life, John tells us, is our love for the brethren, and this flows out of our love for God, which in turn is a direct result of his prior love for us in Christ. For, he writes, "Every one who believes that Jesus is the Christ is a child of God, and every one who loves the parent loves the child" (1 John 5:1). It follows that "by this we know that we love the children of God, when we love God and obey his commandments" (1 John 5:2). That is, when a person comes to know God, who is love, he becomes his child, but not his only child. There are others in the family who have believed upon him also. If then we love the Father, we will love the other children—our brothers—as we love the parent. Or reversed, we know that we really love God if we bear no ill to our brothers but love them from the heart. If we recite creeds and evince no love, we are, says John flatly, liars and no more

(1 John 4:20). That is clearly a restatement of Jesus' constant appeal for the personal unity of intention, words, and acts.

In all their forms, *agapaō* occurs some ninety times and *phileō* over a dozen times in the Johannine writings. It is clear that John thinks of love in three principal ways:

a. It is the Father's love for men in Christ. Undoubtedly the classic teaching in this regard is John 3:16. The greatest verity of the gospel is God's love for men, so great that he sacrificed his son to win them. "In this is love," says John, "not that we loved God but that he loved us and sent his Son to be the expiation for our sins" (1 John 4:10; cf. 4:19; John 13:1).

b. Love produces a reciprocal love from the believer to Christ. As Jesus abides in the Father's love, so are we to abide in his love. And we know that we abide in his love if we keep his commandments (John 14:15, 21; 15:9 f.; 1 John 4:9, 13, 16).

c. Love is communal, it reaches out to all men in Christ. Jesus' commandments are summed up in one: "Even as I have loved you, . . . you love one another" (John 13:34 f.; 15:12, 17); and in 1 John 3:23, "we should believe in the name of his Son Jesus Christ and love one another, just as he has commanded us" (cf. 1 John 2:10; 3:11, 16 f.; 4:7, 11, 20 f.; 5:1). In fine, "we know that we have passed out of death into life, because we love the brethren" (1 John 3:14). Such is the substance of eternal life in Christ.

5. "Eternal life" anticipates a day of perfection. John's eschatology is not altogether "realized." With Paul, John looks forward to a consummation; in this hope both writers are consonant with the teaching of Jesus concerning the kingdom of God and the Son of man. Eternal life is a present possession, a realized blessing, but it remains to be perfected and realized to the full. Evil is to be judged and death destroyed that eternal life may be complete and free from dread and

alienation. The hour is coming, Jesus says (John 5:28 f.), when the righteous will come forth to the resurrection of life, and the unrighteous to the resurrection of judgment. Everyone who believes in the Son shall have eternal life, "and I will raise him up at the last day" (John 6:40). The same saying is repeated in the eucharistic passage of John 6:54. What is this last day as the evangelist understands it?

The answer, R. H. Lightfoot suggests, lies in the story of Lazarus' resurrection which is a sign of the universal resurrection of the future. When Jesus brings Lazarus back to life, "the future is, in a single case, brought into the present; . . . for a single human being that hour, which is to come for every man, now is."[6] Jesus is Lord of life and death. This act of resurrection reveals to Martha not only that he who is Lord of that far off day is Lord here and now but also that this present life in the Lord differs from the future life only in degree, not in kind. Though we have eternal life as a present possession, we are to live in the hope of the last day when all is to be fulfilled. Lazarus lived to die again; and so must we die one day. But, Jesus says, "he who believes in me, *though he die, yet shall he live*" (John 11:25). In the First Letter of John, the writer warns his readers that it is now the last hour (1 John 2:18) when many antichrists have gone out and are working against the truth. But there is hope: "Abide in him, so that when he appears we may have confidence and not shrink from him in shame at his coming" (1 John 2:28). We know for certain that we are God's children now, still "it does not yet appear what we shall be, but we know that when he appears we shall be like him, for we shall see him as he is" (1 John 3:2). Meanwhile, we take hope in the power of the present, aware that while evil appears outwardly to be growing at the same rate as good, it is in reality conquered, for "the darkness is passing away and the true light is already shining" (1 John 2:8). And as the true light continues to shine, we abide in God's love and are continually perfected in it, free of fear, for "there is no fear in love" (1 John 4:18).

In John as in Paul (and the apostolic kerygma of Acts), there is essentially the same proclamation as in Jesus' teaching of the kingdom of God. But here the kingdom is explicitly Christ and life. Eternal life is personal and communal, it is love itself, it anticipates the fulfillment of the last day. For John, the kingdom of God is Christ himself.

1 Peter: Wholeness and Hope in Christ

The same pattern of the apostolic writings appears in this epistle as well. Although the kingdom is never mentioned (except as the royal priesthood, 1 Peter 2:9), there can be no mistake about who and what has taken its place: Christ and the faithful community, his creation. The apostle centers his theology on Christ, to whom he then relates the community of believers; he then pleads for wholeness in the community, and finally proclaims an eschatological hope.

1. Jesus Christ is the kingdom. This cannot be demonstrated directly, but it is an inference that accords well with the Christocentric nature of the apostolic kerygma. The second section of the kerygma outline in Jesus' proclamation ("the kingdom of God is upon you," Mark 1:15) is translated in the apostolic preaching into the concrete event of the redemptive ministry of Jesus himself. He has become the kingdom for the apostles—here too, with one additional change. Where Jesus followed his proclamation of the kingdom with the words "repent and believe the gospel," and the apostles with "repent and be baptized," Peter spurs his hearers on to ethical living rather than to repentance. The reason is obvious, of course, for he is talking to Christians, not to the unconverted. The kerygma can be varied to fit the audience without changing its basic ingredients, as it is in the Sermon on the Mount. In 1 Peter the distinction between *kerygma* and *didachē*

(teaching) becomes very fine indeed. This letter is an excellent example of the flexibility of the kerygma when it is addressed to a community of Christians. In brief, here is how Peter presents the kerygma:

a. The prophecies of the Old Testament have been fulfilled in the suffering and glory of Christ (1 Peter 1:10-12); the stone of stumbling has become the cornerstone (1 Peter 2:4, 6, 8; cf. Ps. 118:22; Isa. 28:16; 8:14 f.).

b. This Jesus
died to deliver his people (1 Peter 1:18 f.; 2:22-24) out of darkness (1 Peter 2:9)

was raised from the dead (1 Peter 1:3, 21; 3:21)

is exalted at God's right hand, with angels, authorities, and powers subject to him (1 Peter 3:22)

and will come again as judge of the wicked and the righteous (1 Peter 4:5, 17).

c. Therefore love the brotherhood (1 Peter 2:17), and "set your hope fully upon the grace that is coming" (1 Peter 1:13).

Inasmuch as the second section agrees with the general apostolic tendency to substitute the ministry of Jesus for the kingdom of God, it seems reasonable to assume that Peter also equates Christ and the kingdom.

2. The community is integrally related to Christ. The expression "in Christ" occurs three times in this letter (1 Peter 3:16; 5:10, 14), but unlike Paul and John, Peter does not hinge his argument on it so much as upon the metaphor of the living stone. Christ, Peter says, quoting Isaiah 28:16, is like a living stone; though rejected of men and a stumbling block, he is nevertheless God's chosen and precious one. Upon this cornerstone, which in its conspicuous position controls

the design of the building, all who believe in Christ are built up as living stones into a spiritual house (1 Peter 2:4-6). This is a remarkable picture of (1) the community's dependence upon Christ and (2) the unity of believers with Christ. Although Peter's metaphor is not given the mystical interpretation that Paul allows his metaphors, it goes without saying that in all essentials it is relating the same truth. Christ is the controlling center who fashions about him a people, integrally related to him and utterly dependent upon him. Peter says that we are "a chosen race, a royal priesthood, a holy nation, God's own people" (1 Peter 2:9), "the flock of God" (1 Peter 5:2); all of which supports the common belief of the apostles that Christ did intend and did create a people of his own. The process by which the community is built up is continually being realized, for they are like newborn babes who after tasting the kindness of the Lord are to continue longing for the pure spiritual milk, "that by it you may *grow up* to salvation" (1 Peter 2:2). Peter knows that salvation is in process of being realized, and in this he is one with Paul and John.

3. The conduct of the community. The fellowship of believers is seen even more clearly in the exhortations to Christlike conduct. Repeatedly Peter urges his readers to stand behind their words with acts and pure intention. These ethical exhortations bear every similarity to Jesus' call for wholeness and fidelity. Christian faith, Peter says, is the commitment of the whole person, or it is nothing. In 1 Peter we find these exhortations:

Gird up your minds (1:13)
Be sober (1:13)
Set your hope ... on grace (1:13)
Be holy in all your conduct (1:15)
Conduct yourselves with fear (1:17)
Love one another earnestly from the heart (1:22)

160

Put away all malice, guile, insincerity, envy, slander (2:1)
Long for the pure spiritual milk (2:2)
Abstain from passions (2:11)
Maintain good conduct (2:12)
Be subject to every human institution (2:13)
Live as free men, yet as servants of God (2:16)
Honor all men (2:17)
Love the brotherhood (2:17)
Fear God (2:17)
Honor the emperor (2:17)
Servants be submissive (2:18)
Wives be submissive (3:1)
Husbands live considerately with your wives (3:7)
Finally, all of you have:

    unity of spirit
    sympathy
    love of the brethren
    a tender heart
    a humble mind (3:8)

Bless (3:9)
Fear not if you suffer for righteousness' sake (3:14)
Nor be troubled (3:14)
Reverence Christ as Lord in your hearts (3:15)
Be prepared, always, to make a defense (3:15)
Keep your conscience clear (3:16)
Arm yourselves (4:1)
Keep sane and sober (4:7)
Hold unfailing love for one another (4:8)
Practice hospitality (4:9)
Employ your gifts for one another (4:10 f.)
Do not be surprised by the proving ordeal (4:12)
But rejoice in so far as you share Christ's sufferings (4:13)
Let none suffer as a wrongdoer (4:15)
Let him not be ashamed who suffers as a Christian (4:16)

Let him glorify God (4:16)
Let those who suffer do right and entrust their souls (4:19)
Tend the flock of God (5:2)
Be subject to the elders (5:5)
Clothe yourself with humility (5:5)
Humble yourselves (5:6)
Cast all your anxieties on him (5:7)
Be sober, be watchful (5:8)
Resist the devil (5:9)
Stand fast in the true grace of God (5:12)

This long catalog of Christian demeanor characterizes Christ-like living which ought to mark all who are in Christ, and therefore in the kingdom of God. Were we asked to sum up this manual of ethics, we could do it in two verses from 1 Peter: First, love toward Christ—"Without having seen him you love him" (1 Peter 1:8); and second, love for others— "love one another earnestly from the heart" (1 Peter 1:22). That is the "code" of the kingdom of God.

Such love for Christ involves participation in his sufferings, even as he had promised his disciples that they would suffer for his sake. Christians must suffer various trials for a little while, Peter says (1 Peter 1:6), in order to prove the genuineness of their faith. As Christ set an example by suffering for us, we are to bear our pains joyfully though we think we suffer unjustly (1 Peter 2:19, 21). As a fellow sufferer (1 Peter 5:1), Peter encourages us to rejoice when we do suffer for righteousness' sake and not be ashamed (1 Peter 4:13, 16; cf. Mark 8:38), for whoever shares Christ's sufferings and is reproached for his name shall be blessed (1 Peter 4:14, 3:14) and shall find "praise and glory and honor at the revelation of Jesus Christ" (1 Peter 1:7). Hence Peter's faith is centered in Jesus' suffering ministry and in the hope of the Lord's return (the Parousia).

4. The hope of perfection. As Jesus' proclamation had its future dimension of hope, so does Peter's. Peter believes that a day will come when all things will be complete, when the community will no longer suffer insult and death. His eschatology can be put succinctly in the words of 1 Peter 1:3-5: By God's "great mercy we have been born anew to a living hope through the resurrection of Jesus Christ from the dead, and to an inheritance which is imperishable, undefiled, and unfading, kept in heaven for you, who by God's power are guarded through faith for a salvation ready to be revealed in the last time." That is process eschatology: it is realized in the past event of Christ's resurrection through which we have been born anew (*anagennēsas*); it is in process of being realized in a hope which continues to live (*elpida zōsan*) and in which we are continually guarded (*phrouroumenous*); and it is yet to be realized in the last time (*en kairō eschatō*), which is genuinely futurist eschatology.

"Hope" as verb and noun occurs four times in 1 Peter and is related in every instance to the fulfillment of history at Christ's appearing. The living hope of 1 Peter 1:3 has already been noted. In 1 Peter 1:13 Christians are urged to "gird up your minds, be sober, set your hope fully upon the grace that is coming to you at the revelation of Jesus Christ." Edward Selwyn is certainly correct when he points to the similarity of this passage to Luke 12:22-40, Q, where the disciples are told to pursue the heavenly, to ply their energy toward seeking the kingdom (Luke 12:31), and to be watchful for the return of the master from the marriage feast, "for the Son of man is coming at an hour you do not expect" (Luke 12:40).[7] The highest goal is the kingdom of God in Jesus' proclamation; for Peter it is Christ. The transposition from the kingdom to Christ is unmistakable. The hope of a future consummation rests ultimately in God, because he has raised Christ from the dead and given him glory (1 Peter 1:21). Hence past, present, and future are contingent upon one another. The past event of the resurrection works forward to give us confidence that salvation will be completed, and the future hope works back upon the present, authenticating the past and supporting our confidence in the total drama of salvation.[8] God speaks from the past into the present, and from the future into the present.

The tension between the now and the not yet, which is characteristic of Jesus' understanding of time, is continued in Peter's eschatological understanding. The future belongs to God, and that is sufficient to release us to the present where we may live freely and creatively. There is no speculation upon the details of the future. Like Jesus, Peter simply claims it as God's time:

Salvation is to be revealed in the last time (1 Peter 1:5).

Praise, glory, and honor are to come at the revelation of Jesus Christ (1 Peter 1:7; cf. the day of the Son of man, Luke 17:30, Q; Matt. 25:31-46, M).

Set your hope upon the grace that is coming to you at the revelation of Jesus Christ (1 Peter 1:13).

They will give account to him who is ready to judge the living and the dead (1 Peter 4:5).

The end of all things is at hand (1 Peter 4:7). Perhaps a better translation would be "the end of all things *has begun*" (*ēggiken*). "It *is* the last hour," says John (1 John 2:18). The future is already working in the present, and the present is moving inexorably toward the future which belongs to God.

The glory ... is to be revealed (1 Peter 5:1).

When the chief Shepherd is manifested you will obtain the unfading crown of glory (1 Peter 5:4).

Humble yourselves that in due time he may exalt you (1 Peter 5:6).

164

God will himself restore, establish, and strengthen you (1 Peter 5:10). This is parallel in thought to 1 Peter 1:6-9 and refers to the complete restoration which is to come at the Parousia.

In conclusion: The kerygma of 1 Peter is consistent with the proclamation of the other apostolic writers in replacing the metaphor of the kingdom with the person of Jesus Christ. Peter also accords with their emphasis upon the community of believers in Christ, whom he illustrates in the metaphor of living stones built upon the Living Stone. The fidelity of personal intention, words, and acts is also uppermost in Peter's theology. This fidelity is fundamentally love of Christ and love of the brethren. Finally, in Peter we discover the same process eschatology which characterizes the rest of the New Testament, and which finds its origin in Jesus' proclamation of the kingdom of God.

Hebrews: the Kingdom, the Priest, and the Community

In this letter the identification of Christ and the kingdom is as unmistakable as it is in the other apostolic writings. The author has the same tendency to substitute Christ for the kingdom; he understands Christ's priestly work in relationship to the community of believers; faith, love, and hope (the highest expressions of Christian conduct) distinguish the community; and the present work of Christ anticipates a perfection which lies in God's future.

1. The kingdom of God is Christ himself. The apostolic kerygma is very plainly outlined in this letter to the Hebrews. Typically, the second section proclaims the person of Christ in place of the kingdom of God (cf. Mark 1:15, the primitive kerygma of Jesus):

a. The prophecies are fulfilled and the new age has dawned (Heb. 1:1-3; 11:40; 2:5; cf. Heb. 2:9; 6:5; 9:9).

b. Jesus the Son, born of David's line, has come (Heb. 7:14), who died for our sins according to the Scriptures (Heb. 1:3; 2:9, 14 f.; 9:14 f., 28; 10:10, 12; 13:12);

was raised from the dead (Heb. 13:20);

has been exalted at the right hand of God (Heb. 1:3; 4:14; 6:20; 8:1; 10:12; 12:2);

and will come again as savior and judge (Heb. 9:27 f.; 10:25-31, 37; 12:25-27).

c. Therefore let us hold fast our confession and go forth unto him (Heb. 4:14; 13:13).

Two appearances of the word kingdom in this letter confirm the equation of Christ and the kingdom of God. In the first, the kingdom belongs to the Son:

But of the Son he says,
"Thy throne, O God, is for ever and ever,
the righteous scepter is the scepter of thy kingdom."
—Hebrews 1:8

In the second, the unshakable kingdom which we have received follows upon the words "Mount Zion . . . city of the living God, the heavenly Jerusalem, . . . the assembly of the first-born who are enrolled in heaven, . . . and to a judge who is God . . . the spirits of just men made perfect, and to Jesus, the mediator of a new covenant" (Heb. 12:22-24). To all these we have come (Heb. 12:22): "Therefore let us be grateful for receiving a kingdom that cannot be shaken" (Heb. 12:28). It seems reasonably clear from this that by the word kingdom the author of Hebrews means both Christ and the community of saints.

2. Jesus is the priest of the new community. Jesus Christ is the high priest who has come to make full and final atone-

166

ment for the sins of his people. He has brought in the new age in which all the typology of the Old Testament is fulfilled. That is the leitmotiv of the letter. We mark these contrasts:

Old Covenant	*New Covenant*
• An earthly tabernacle	• A heavenly tabernacle
• The high priest in the Holy Place	• Jesus in the Holy Place
• Entered once a year	• Entered once for all
• Offered the blood of animals	• Offered his own blood
• The priest needed the sacrifice for himself	• Christ was without blemish
• The offering purified only the flesh	• Christ's offering purges the conscience

The purpose of Christ's priestly office is to create a body of people whose characteristic is wholeness. In the same sense that he is king over the realm of the righteous, he is priest of his people. Both imply a community, as can be seen from these illustrations from the Letter to the Hebrews:

a. We are sons who are brought to glory (2:10) and chastened because he loves us (12:5-8).
b. We are God's children (2:13 f.).
c. And therefore we are Christ's brethren (2:11 f.; 3:1, 12).
d. Because he loves the true descendants of Abraham, he has become like us in human form in order to expiate our sins as high priest (2:16 f.).
e. We are God's house, built by him (3:2-6; cf. the new house of Israel, 8:8, 10).
f. We are sharers *(metochoi)* of Christ (3:14), of the Holy Spirit (6:4), and of the heavenly call (3:1).
g. Jesus is the source of eternal salvation to all who obey him (5:9).

h. He has gone into the inner shrine as a forerunner on our behalf, having become a high priest for ever in the succession of Melchizedek (6:20).

i. He is able to save absolutely those who draw near to God through him, since he always lives to make intercession for them (7:25; 10:14).

j. He is the mediator of a new covenant, so that those who are called may receive the promised eternal inheritance (9:15; 10:16).

k. He appears in the presence of God in our behalf (9:24).

l. He is the great shepherd of the sheep (13:20).

The importance of the faithful community is an integral part of his theology.

3. The fidelity of the community. The writer of Hebrews exhorts his readers to seek that personal wholeness which is the distinctive mark of the disciples of Jesus Christ. Observe how often he repeats the exhortation "Let us . . ." (hortatory subjunctive):

Consider Jesus, the apostle and high priest of our confession (3:1)
Exhort one another (3:13)
Do not harden your hearts (3:8, 15)
Let us fear lest you fall (4:1)
Let us strive to enter that rest (4:11)
Let us hold fast our confession (4:14)
Let us draw near to the throne of grace (4:16)
Let us go on to maturity (6:1)
Let us draw near in faith (10:22)
Let us hold fast the confession of our hope (10:23)
Let us stir up one another to love (10:24)
Do not throw away your confidence (10:35)
Let us lay aside every weight (12:1)
Let us run the race with perseverance (12:1)

Consider him who endured such hostility from sinners (12:3)

Lift your drooping hands, and strengthen your weak knees (12:12)

Make straight paths for your feet (12:13)

Strive for peace with all men (12:14)

See to it that no one fail to obtain the grace of God (12:15)

Do not refuse him who is speaking (12:25)

Let us be grateful (12:28)

Let brotherly love continue (13:1)

Do not neglect to show hospitality to strangers (13:2)

Remember those in prison, and those ill-treated (13:3)

Let marriage be held in honor, and the marriage bed be undefiled (13:4)

Keep your life free from love of money (13:5)

Remember and obey your leaders (13:7, 17)

Do not be led away by strange teachings (13:9)

Let us go forth to him outside the camp (13:13)

Do not neglect to do good and to share what you have (13:16)

We may sum up these exhortations under three headings: faith, love, and hope.

a. Faith. By faith we enter the community: "Let us draw near with a true heart in full assurance of faith, with our hearts sprinkled clean" (Heb. 10:22). By faith we shall live and keep our souls (Heb. 10:38 f.), for "faith is the assurance of things hoped for, the conviction of things not seen" (Heb. 11:1). After presenting the magnificent hymn of faith in chapter 11, the author then exhorts his readers to lay aside every besetting weight, "looking to Jesus the pioneer and perfecter of our faith" (Heb. 12:2). Thus faith is completely bound up with the origin and the goal of that faith—Christ. Getting to know him by faith is like entering the kingdom of God.

b. Love. Yet entering the kingdom is also a communal experience, and always shows its power in love for others. We are told to consider how to stir up one another to love and good works, to encourage each other, not neglecting to meet together (Heb. 10:24 f.). We are to let brotherly love continue, showing hospitality to strangers, prisoners, and the down-and-out (Heb. 13:1-3), doing good and sharing what we have (Heb. 13:16). We are to exhort one another (Heb. 3:13), and to the best of our ability see to it that no one fails to obtain the grace of God (Heb. 12:15).

c. Hope. The author shares the kerygmatic understanding of time, with its dimensions of past, present, and future. His faith is characterized by hope, but by a hope that makes every word and act in the present of ultimate importance. It is extremely important, he tells us, to grasp the future through the living of the present. There is an "if" about living in Christ:

"We are his house *if (ean)* we hold fast our confidence and pride in our hope" (Heb. 3:6).
"For we share in Christ, *if only (eanper)* we hold our first confidence firm to the end" (Heb. 3:14).

He writes with urgency that we may come to realize "the full assurance of hope until the end" (Heb. 6:11), and that we may continue to encourage one another, "and all the more as you see the Day drawing near" (Heb. 10:25). It will be but a little while before "the coming one shall come and shall not tarry" (Heb. 10:37), when he who was "offered once to bear the sins of many, will appear a second time, not to deal with sin but to save those who are eagerly waiting for him" (Heb. 9:28; cf. Heb. 10:27-31). Then we shall enter the blessedness of God's rest (*katapausis,* cf. Heb. 3:11, 18; 4:1, 3, 5, 9-11).

This "rest in God" is a hope that has sustained generations of Christians and inspired the most articulate expressions of faith. Augustine prays, "O Lord, Thou hast made us for thyself, and our heart is restless until it rests in thee." And George Herbert, in a poem of exquisite beauty, "The Pulley," describes the believer's "pull" toward the rest which God alone can give to man:

> When God at first made man,
> Having a glass of blessings standing by;
> Let us (said He) pour on him all we can:
> Let the world's riches, which dispersèd lie,
> Contract into a span.
>
> So strength first made a way;
> Then beauty flowed, then wisdom, honour, pleasure:
> When almost all was out, God made a stay,
> Perceiving that alone of all His treasure
> Rest in the bottom lay.
>
> For if I should (said He)
> Bestow this jewel also on My creature,
> He would adore My gifts instead of Me,
> And rest in Nature, not the God of Nature.
> So both should losers be.
>
> Yet let him keep the rest,
> But keep them with repining restlessness:
> Let him be rich and weary, that at least,
> If goodness lead him not, yet weariness
> May toss him to My breast.

Faith, love, and rest in Christ: these are distinctive of the author's belief. And Jesus placed them at the center of his own ministry.

READINGS ON CHAPTER SIX

Bultmann, Rudolf. *Das Evangelium des Johannes*. Göttingen: Vandenhoeck & Ruprecht, 1962.
Denney, James. *Jesus and the Gospel*. London: Hodder and Stoughton, 1908.

Dodd, C. H. *The Apostolic Preaching and Its Developments.* London: Hodder and Stoughton, 1936.

―――. *Historical Tradition in the Fourth Gospel.* Cambridge: Cambridge University Press, 1963.

Forsyth, P. T. *The Person and Place of Jesus Christ.* London: Independent Press, 1955.

Hartshorne, Charles. *The Logic of Perfection and Other Essays in Neoclassical Metaphysics.* La Salle, Ill.: Open Court Publishing Co., 1962.

Lightfoot, R. H. *St. John's Gospel.* Oxford: Oxford University Press, 1956.

Manson, William. *The Epistle to the Hebrews.* London: Hodder and Stoughton, 1951.

Munck, Johannes. *Paul and the Salvation of Mankind.* Richmond: John Knox Press, 1959.

Nygren, Anders. *Agape and Eros.* Translated by Philip S. Watson. Philadelphia: Westminster Press, 1953.

Selwyn, E. G. *The First Epistle of St. Peter.* London: Macmillan, 1958.

CHAPTER SEVEN

The
Metaphors of Christ
and the
Kingdom

THUS FAR this study has dealt with a number of New Testament metaphors which figure significantly in the teaching of Jesus and his interpreters. In each of them Jesus Christ is the source of life, the one to whom the community of believers is intimately related. It will be well to bring these metaphors together and add several new ones that are of considerable importance in understanding the relationship of Jesus Christ, the kingdom of God, and personal existence.

New Testament Metaphors

1. The kingdom of God. At the center of this primary metaphor is Jesus Christ, the personalization of the kingship of God, whose subjects comprise the realm of God in all its diversity. The kingdom is a metaphor of the one and the many.

2. The Son of man. From Daniel 7 Jesus has taken a figure of the diverse community, the saints of the Most High, and incorporated its symbolism in his person. He calls the twelve and appeals to every man to follow him. Through his redeeming activity he forms the corporate Son of man and shares his authority with men. Alone, Jesus is the personal embodiment

of the Son of man (the one); in him his followers become the Son of man (the many in one).

3. The living water and streams of living water (John 4: 14; 7:37 f.). Jesus is the living water (the one), of whom if any drink, "Out of his heart shall flow rivers of living water" (the one in many).

4. The bread and the partakers (John 6:27-58). Jesus is the bread of life (the one), and those who eat of him shall never hunger (the many in one).

5. Light and lights (John 8:12; 9:5; 12:35; Matt. 5:14). Jesus is the source of light, and when men share in that light they become the light of the world (the one in many).

6. The door and the shepherd of the sheep (John 10:1-16). This figure points to the utter dependence of the sheep upon the shepherd who is both the entrance to life (the door) and the guide and sustainer of life (the shepherd). There is a sense of oneness in the words, "the good shepherd lays down his life for the sheep," and "there shall be one flock, one shepherd" (John 10:11, 16). The same idea is expressed indirectly in John 11:52, where Jesus is to die "to gather into one the children of God who are scattered abroad." We should also compare 1 Peter 5:4, where Jesus is the chief shepherd; Hebrews 13:20, where he is the great shepherd of the sheep; Revelation 7:17, "the Lamb in the midst of the throne will be their shepherd"; and the beautiful passage in Isaiah 40:11:

> He will feed his flock like a shepherd
>   he will gather the lambs in his arms,
> he will carry them in his bosom,
>   and gently lead those that are with young.

(Cf. Ezek. 34:11-16; Jer. 50:6, 17.)

7. The true vine and the branches (John 15:1-11). In one of the most intimate of the nature metaphors, Jesus compares himself to the vine (the one) and his followers to the branches

which make up the vine (the many in one). Jesus is not only the root and stem of the vine, but the whole of it, branches and all. This relationship he explains as a mutual indwelling: we abide in him and he in us ("as the branch cannot bear fruit by itself, unless it abides in the vine, neither can you, unless you abide in me," John 15:4-7; cf. 6:56). The Old Testament background to this metaphor is worth keeping in mind, for there it is also bound up with the community (Israel) which has been planted by Yahweh. But from there on, the analogy differs, for Israel has degenerated as a wild vine (Jer. 2:21; 12:10; Ezek. 15:2-8; 19:10-14; Hos. 10:1; cf. Ps. 80:8 ff.); there Yahweh has planted it, but Jesus identifies himself with it. He draws a lesson from this symbol of corporate fellowship. It is the importance of symbiosis between branches and vine; otherwise, he says, the branches will wither and bear no fruit (John 15:6). In the Gospel According to John, the Father is to the Son as the Son is to us. This theme of mutual indwelling is presented once again in John 15:8-10 and repeated more fully in chapter 17. The élan in both relationships is love and fullness of joy.

John's metaphor of the vine allows a comparison with the figure of the olive tree in Romans 11:16-24. There, new branches (the Gentiles) have been grafted into the tree in place of the old ones which have been broken off (Israel). There are minor differences in detail, but John and Paul are quite in accord that to live is to dwell in Christ. In Paul's metaphor and in John's, Jesus is the whole olive tree, he is the source and sustainer of all its life (the one in many), and the branches are an integral part of the tree (the many in one). This theology of indwelling is panentheistic: all things find their life in God, and he participates in the life of all things. The analogy is a powerful one, for it compels us to think of God and his creatures as a cosmic organism, whose vital force is the symbiosis of love.

8. The body of Christ. Paul's great metaphor of the body

expresses the cosmic organism through the analogy of persons, who are one in many. Paul's expressions "in Christ" and "with Christ" may now be incorporated in the magnificent symbol of "one body in Christ."

In the classical passage of 1 Corinthians 12, Paul is concerned with the relation of believers to Christ and to one another. The unity and diversity of the body is beautifully expressed in verse 12; Christ is the whole of the body (one in many), while each member has his own individual function within the body (many in one): "For just as the body is one and has many members, and all the members of the body, though many, are one body, so it is with Christ" (1 Cor. 12: 12). It is not a pantheism. Christ maintains his particularity of lordship, and we our individuality so that we are not absorbed into him. In some mysterious manner, best explained as the vitality of love, we experience a unity in diversity.

It is the Spirit who has baptized us all in Christ: "For by one Spirit we were all baptized into one body—Jews or Greeks, slaves or free—and all were made to drink of one Spirit" (1 Cor. 12:13). It is God who adjusts the body and distributes the parts with honor, "that there may be no discord in the body" (1 Cor. 12:24 f.). The Holy Spirit adds and waters, the Father adjusts and harmonizes, the Son *is* the body.

In Colossians the figure is rather more elaborate as Paul presents Christ as the head of the body. That is an important development of the metaphor because it guards against any pantheistic tendency to depreciate the lordship of Christ over the body. In Colossians 1:17 f. Paul makes special mention of the preexistence and unifying power of Christ: "He is before all things, and in him all things hold together. He is the head of the body, the church; he is the beginning, the first-born from the dead, that in everything he might be preeminent." For without the head there can be no life, no growth; therefore we are to hold fast to the head, "from whom the whole body, nourished and knit together through its joints and liga-

176

ments, grows with a growth that is from God" (Col. 2:19). Here he expresses the unity of believers with the head and the unity of one believer to another, and all with all, who are nourished and knit together.

Christ the head, and the interrelation of believers and their growth together, are reiterated in Ephesians 4:15 f., a tremendous passage that has already figured in this study: "Rather, speaking the truth in love, we are to grow up in every way into him who is the head, into Christ, from whom the whole body, joined and knit together by every joint with which it is supplied, when each part is working properly, makes bodily growth and upbuilds itself in love." Here there is diversity in the lordship of Christ, unity in the dependence of the parts to Christ and to one another (Eph. 4:25, 2:16, 3:6), and bodily growth in love. Like the kingdom of God and the Son of man, the body of Christ is something which grows; it is a process, an eschatological process of divine love. Its object and its effect is to bring harmony and sociality into the cosmos —the body of God.

9. The building in Christ. The metaphor of the building is a favorite one among the biblical writers. We find it in Psalm 89:4; Ruth 4:11; Isaiah 28:16; Jeremiah 12:16 f.; 31: 4-6; Amos 9:11; John 2:19; 1 Peter 2:5. Paul begins with the foundation stone which is Christ (1 Cor. 3:9-17), who alone serves as the foundation of the building. In Ephesians 2:20, Christ is the *chief* cornerstone, since the foundation consists also of the apostles and prophets of the New Testament era who, like Paul, have laid the foundation of Christ, and are accordingly considered part of the foundation themselves. Upon this foundation *(themelios)*, we, the building of God *(theou oikodomē)*, are built up stone by stone as members of a unit. The metaphor reveals the particularity of Christ as Lord, and the individuality of each stone, yet it stresses the unity of the building as a whole. Whether *akrogōniaios* refers to the corner of the foundation, as is usually supposed, or to the keystone

of the arch which holds the edifice together, the crucial position of Christ is clear. Perhaps Paul had both positions in mind—Christ as the foundation *and* as the locking keystone of the completed edifice. Together, the cornerstone and the keystone symbolize the kerygmatic truth that Christ is the beginning, the body, and the completion of our faith: "I am the Alpha and the Omega, . . . who is and who was and who is to come, the Almighty" (Rev. 1:8; cf. 21:6 the beginning and the end; 22:13 the first and the last). "In him all things hold together" (Col. 1:17). To sum it all up in Paul's own words: it is Christ "in whom the whole structure is joined together and grows into a holy temple in the Lord" (Eph. 2:21). The two verbal expressions "grows" and "being built up" are consonant with the concept of divine process. For the building and the body of Christ are still in process of growing: inwardly, as they grow stronger in individual faith and intention; and outwardly, as men take their places of membership like living stones being built into a spiritual house (1 Peter 2:5). One by one, by divine grace they are fitly joined together in the Lord, so that Christ, the separate and sustaining foundation and keystone, is also the whole building in and with us. This is a magnificent model not only of the church but also of the whole universe, which has its existence in God. The analogy is surpassed only by the intimacy of the body metaphor and the symbolism of marriage.

10. The bride of Christ. Like the metaphor of the building, the figure of the bride and bridegroom is a popular one in biblical tradition. God's relationship to Israel is likened to the intimate marriage of a husband and wife (Hos. 1–3; Isa. 54:1-8; 61:10; 62:4 f.; Ezek. 16; 23). In the New Testament, Jesus is the bridegroom and his people the bride. In Mark 2:18-20 Jesus remarks that fasting is inappropriate for his disciples because the bridegroom is with them (cf. John 3:29). The kingdom of God is also compared to a marriage feast (Matt. 22:1-14, M; cf. Luke 14:16-24, Q; 12:35-37, Q), and

to the ten maidens awaiting the bridegroom's return (Matt. 25:1-13, M).

Paul elaborates upon the imagery in Ephesians 5:23-33 where Christ's relation to the church is employed to illustrate the ethical relationship of husbands and wives. The figure of the head and the body is used again, but here the head is the husband; and the church, his body, is the wife. Through the passage there runs the thread of fidelity, purity, and love: be subject as the church is subject—as Christ loved the church—that he might sanctify her—that she might be holy and without blemish—nourish, love.

There is no question in Paul's mind that Christ and the church are already married (realized eschatology); he is using the fact of this marriage to exhort his readers to the same standards of fidelity in their personal marriages. But it is also true that the present church can hardly be described in such glowing terms as "presented in splendor, without spot or wrinkle or any such thing, holy and without blemish" (Eph. 5:27). Here is that tension between present and future which is so typical of New Testament faith. The church is indeed married, but she is not yet perfectly whole and will not be until the consummation. Paul phrases Ephesians 5:25 f. carefully enough not to leave himself open to the charge of defying reality. Christ, he says, has given himself for the church and cleansed her, but he has done this that he might sanctify her, that the church *might* be presented before him without blemish. In these Greek *hina* clauses Paul is saying that Christ's present ministry is a sanctification now in process. He says much the same thing to the church at Corinth when he writes, "I betrothed you to Christ to present you as a pure bride to her one husband. But . . ." (2 Cor. 11:2). He acknowledges that the church is not now pure. That is why Christ "continues to nourish it up to maturity" *(ektrephō)*, why he "fosters it with warm and tender care" *(thalpō*; Eph. 5:29). And, too, it is why in the book of Revelation the church is said to be married to the Lamb precisely at the Parousia (Rev. 19:7-9; 21:2, 9; 22:17). As the kingdom can be said to be here and not here, present but not in perfection, so the church is both married and yet to be married. The bride awaits the consummation when her purity will be perfected, when she will literally be holy and without blemish. Meanwhile, the relation of the bride to Christ is one of progressive purification.

The analogy of Christ's relationship to the church was one that lay well to hand for Paul's ethical admonitions to the husbands and wives of Ephesus. Paul's understanding of our life in Christ as a marriage is an inspired analogy, for of all the metaphors it is the most elementally expressive of the love which holds us together. It is a metaphor of sociality, in which two persons become "we" in "I" and "thou": "The two shall become one. This is a great mystery, and I take it to mean Christ and the church" (Eph. 5:31 f.).

11. The church of God. Each of the metaphors considered so far is a model taken from ordinary experience and familiar to us all. God is concretely present in every one of them; hence the evangelists and apostles find a point of contact in every analogy and heighten them to the cosmic level of Christ. They all point to the underlying reality that Christ is the source of life in whom men become new creations and a new people. All the metaphors share with the analogy of the kingdom of God two central themes: Jesus Christ is the life-giving Lord and King; we are the life-receiving realm. Now this is also true of the church. The church comprises the lordship of Christ over his people, and his unity with them as a community. In every word used by Jesus and the apostles to describe God's relation to the community of believers there is the concept of a realm on the one hand, and his transcendent lordship or kingship on the other. That has been borne out clearly in the metaphors of the kingdom of God, the Son of man, the living water, the bread of life, the door and shepherd of the sheep, the light and lights, the vine and the branches,

the head and the body, the corner-keystone and the building, the husband and the bride.

The church is no exception. In its classical meaning, ecclesia is the assembly of a summoned people. It means literally, "those who are called out." In the Old and New Testaments it is given a distinctively theistic setting; it becomes the church *of God (ecclēsia tou theou)*.[1] The church is always understood to be the assembly *of God*. Apart from God's calling and his lordship in Christ, the assembly has no existence; it is an assembly of people created by the Lord and belonging to the Lord (a genitive of the author and possessor). In this sense the church is a synonym for all the other metaphors, including the kingdom of God. The Lord of the assembly is the King who exercises his reign and who personifies the kingdom. The assembly of those who are called out by the Lord is identical to the realm of the kingdom.

Ecclesia in the New Testament

Let us look briefly at the use of the term ecclesia in the New Testament, and the synonyms which some of the evangelists substitute for it.

1. The book of Acts. The word ecclesia appears for the first time in Acts 5:11 and 8:1, 3, where we read of the congregation gathered about the apostles at Jerusalem. The people are Christians (Acts 2:37-42), for they have repented at the words of the apostles, have been baptized for the forgiveness of sins, and received the gift of the Holy Spirit. That is important, for no one becomes a *conscious* member of Christ's body until he first believes in him; and that is equally true of the kingdom of God and the other metaphors.

In the whole of the New Testament the relationship of a believer and of all believers to Christ is one of intersubjectivity and corporate personality. Accordingly there is no such thing as an isolated Christian. Wherever he is, there the church is as a whole. And wherever there is a local congregation, there the whole church is also present. The adjective "whole" in Acts 5:11 and 15:22 attests this concept of the corporate personality of the church.

2. The Pauline Epistles. In the Pauline writings the church is also a corporate unity. In 1 Corinthians 12:28, the universal church is comprised of many members; in 1 Corinthians 14:23 and Romans 16:23 we find the expression "the whole church." There are also local manifestations of the one church: Corinth, 1 Corinthians 1:2, 2 Corinthians 1:1; Cenchreae, Romans 16:1; Thessalonica, 1 Thessalonians 1:1, 2 Thessalonians 1:1 (cf. Col. 4:15 f.; 1 Cor. 4:17). Then, too, there are the local assemblies which are met especially for worship (1 Cor. 11: 18; 14:19, 23, 28, 34 f.). None of these passages refers to a local church—say, the Corinthian church—but always to the church of God as it is in Corinth. Sometimes Paul speaks in the plural of the churches in Asia (1 Cor. 16:19); Judaea (1 Thess. 2:14; Gal. 1:22); Macedonia (2 Cor. 8:1); Galatia (1 Cor. 16:1); and of all the churches (1 Cor. 7:17; 11:16; 14:33; Rom. 16:16; 2 Cor. 8:18-19, 23). But the churches are always the church because of their communion with Christ, and this can only mean that ecclesiology and Christology are intimately related: "Christ is the ecclesia itself, since the latter is 'the body of Christ.' But then again he is also above the Church, being its head. Such statements are closely inter-related. Christology and ecclesiology are obviously on the same footing."[2] That is certainly the way Paul understands it, for he writes in Romans 16:16 and Galatians 1:22 of Christ's congregations, and in 1 Thessalonians 2:14 of the congregations in Judaea, God's people in Jesus Christ. On this relationship R. H. Fuller remarks that

Paul does not speak of a Christian church or congregation side by side of other churches, Jewish or pagan, but of the assembly *of God in Christ*. The Church is the Messianic community. It is not an assembly of men initiated by their own volition, it origi-

182

nates in . . . Christ and lives through its unity with the Messiah in his death and resurrection and through the indwelling of his Spirit.[3]

But this can be said as well of the realm of the kingdom, which is nothing without the reign of Christ who personifies the kingdom. It could also be said of every other metaphor of fellowship.

3. The Johannine Writings. John has no trace of the ecclesia in his theology—strange indeed, unless there are other metaphors which take its place. That is what has happened. In place of the church and the kingdom we find the metaphors of light, bread, water, the shepherd and his flock, the vine and the branches—all of which are life-giving. They all bear the same meaning.

4. 1 Peter. The word ecclesia does not appear here either. But again there are synonyms for the metaphor: the flock of God, the house of God, a royal priesthood, the people of God. These we have already found to be synonyms of the kingdom of God. Although neither the kingdom nor the church is mentioned directly, there are ample metaphors that serve as surrogates.

5. Hebrews. Only one of the two occurrences of ecclesia in Hebrews interests us here (in the other, Heb. 12:23, the scene is set in the heavenly Jerusalem; but even there it bears the sense of the realm of God). In the first, Hebrews 2:12, the author quotes from Psalm 22:22: "I will proclaim thy name to my brethren, in the midst of the congregation I will praise thee"; he then follows with a quotation from Isaiah 8:18: "Here am I, and the children God has given me." The imagery is similar to the New Testament church, for the people of God (his children) are "given" to Christ.

There are other churchly strains running through the letter. We are God's house in Christ (Heb. 3:2-6) and partners of Christ and sharers of the Holy Spirit (Heb. 3:14; 6:4). Christ has died for us his people (Heb. 6:20; 7:25; 9:15). He is the great shepherd of the sheep (Heb. 13:20). All these metaphors apply equally to the kingdom of God as well as to the church of God.

A dangerous equation perhaps? Traditional theology separates the transcendent kingdom of God from the earthly church, and speaks of the church visible, and the church invisible and triumphant.

That is the usual distinction, and it recognizes that there is a discrepancy between the ideal kingdom and the reality of the institution called the church. The contention here is that the kingdom of God and the church of God (note the full expression) are identical in the sense that they share these characteristics with all the other figures:

(a) They are eschatological metaphors. The kingdom of God, for both Jesus and the early church, is divine grace which has power to make men whole. It has come, it continually comes, it is yet to come. This is also the case with the church of God. It too has its three time dimensions.

(b) They are existential metaphors, symbols of God's *concrete* activity in every moment of time. The divine perfection of the kingdom and the church is an abstraction, like the love and goodness of God. In an abstract sense God is always loving and just by nature. He is the King of the kingdom and the God of the church—yesterday, today, and forever. But the concrete ways in which God creatively exhibits his perfection from moment to moment are *how* he exists and manifests his power to heal the nations. Thus there are two dimensions of God's existence, and a distinction needs to be made between the universality of God and the particularity of God, between his transcendent, abstract goodness, and his goodness as he realizes it in particular situations.[4] Accordingly, the kingdom of God and the church of God share these two divine dimensions: they are always ideal potentialities, and partially realized actualities.

(c) They are metaphors of process. God realizes his perfect universal love in the concrete events of time, and that means that his desire to fellowship with all men and to call them into his wholeness depends upon their freedom to respond to his call or to alienate themselves from him. Therefore, the concrete kingdom and church is always imperfectly realized and is always in process of realization. Jesus felt the tension of the now and the not yet of the kingdom. So did the earliest Christians. And so do we.

(d) They are metaphors of participation. Persons are not absorbed into God; they are intersubjectively related to him. God calls them into being and sustains them, and in their individuality they contribute to his experience. Nothing in the universe can be defined as it is "in itself," for everything is interrelated with everything else as inextricably as the parts of the body belong to every other part. God and the kingdom, Christ and the church are inseparable.

(e) They are cosmic metaphors. Since God is the ground of all wholeness, it is correct to say that wherever we find words and acts of wholeness, there God is present. And where God is present in the creativity of men, there the Christ of the kingdom and the church is present. Frederick Denison Maurice once remarked that Christ "is in every man, the source of all light that ever visits him, the root of all the righteous thoughts and acts that he is ever able to conceive or do."[5] That is a magnificent expression of Christian faith. The proclamation of Jesus Christ is not merely one historic event among others, but the declaration that God in Christ is the ground of all creativity in the universe. Jesus saw the kingdom wherever he found love and fidelity, and we may find the church wherever we see acts of healing and purity of language.

What then of the institutional church? Its role is to proclaim Jesus Christ who has personalized God in his ministry of teaching, healing, suffering, and resurrection; to call men out of forgetfulness to him in whom they live and move and have their being. The institutional church is the earthen vessel which bears the treasure the people of God offer in Christ's name to the world. The sole justification of the church as an institution is to live the life of Christlike wholeness and to call the world in word and act to consciousness of him. To be is to be together in God. Every metaphor of the kingdom proclaims that tremendous fact.

READINGS ON CHAPTER SEVEN

Best, Ernest. *One Body in Christ*. London: S.P.C.K., 1955.

Hartshorne, Charles. *The Logic of Perfection and Other Essays in Neoclassical Metaphysics*. La Salle, Ill.: Open Court Publishing Co., 1962.

Maurice, Frederick Denison. *Theological Essays*. New York: Harper & Row, 1957.

Richardson, Alan. (ed.). *A Theological Word Book of the Bible*. London: SCM Press, 1954.

Robinson, John A. T. *The Body: A Study in Pauline Theology* ("Studies in Biblical Theology," No. 5.) London: SCM Press, 1953.

Schmidt, Karl Ludwig. *The Church*. Translated by J. R. Coates. London: Adam and Charles Black, 1950.

Thornton, L. S. *The Common Life in the Body of Christ*. London: Dacre Press, 1944.

CHAPTER EIGHT

The
Kingdom of God
and the
Consummation

BIBLICAL FAITH has had a futuristic perspective since the days of the prophets, who told of the coming activity of God. In the writings of the Qumran sect, in the teaching of John the Baptist, in the ministry of Jesus, and the writings of the earliest Christians, eschatology is always preeminent. Jesus proclaimed the inauguration of the new time in his person, but he anticipated a day of fulfillment which was yet to come in the future. The early church looked back to what God had accomplished in Jesus Christ; they felt his power at work in the present; but they were full of expectation for what God was about to do in the future when their Lord returned. The three dimensions of New Testament eschatology are succinctly present in the Pauline formula of the Lord's Supper: "For as often as you eat this bread and drink the cup, you proclaim the Lord's death until he comes" (1 Cor. 11:26). Present proclamation, remembrance of the Lord's passion, anticipation of his return—these are the rudiments of apostolic theology.

Yet if there is anything of this theology that is offensive to modern men and their belief in progress, it is the New Testament teaching of the apparently world-shattering fulfillment of the kingdom at the return of Christ. Men do not claim the earth, nor do they build kingdoms and highways if they expect an imminent end to history. Jesus seemed to live in this expectation, and the early Christians as well.

But is it the promise of God's activity in the future or the *manner* of his activity that offends us? It is the manner, not the hope itself. For our culture is thoroughly eschatological: we believe in the future and its promises. Everything we undertake is begun with a goal (or *eschaton*) in view. Biblical faith has affected our life to this extent at least, that we are a thoroughly eschatological people.

The question, then, is what sort of futurist eschatology? Do those present-day apocalyptists who denigrate this world in preparation for the next genuinely carry on the New Testament tradition? We should do a grave injustice to the biblical understanding of time to say that. Earlier this study showed that for the Old Testament prophets, beginning with Amos and Hosea, the eschatological promise had nothing to do with the end of history and time, but instead with the future activity of God in history. God's future acts will be as decisive as his great acts in the past. Hosea anticipates a new entry into the promised land, Isaiah foretells of a new David and a new Zion, Jeremiah proclaims the coming of a new covenant, Second Isaiah prophesies the new exodus. The focus of their message is more upon the future than upon the past, but it is the fulfillment *of history* they foretell, not its destruction.[1]

Jesus and the early church proclaim that the time anticipated by the prophets has dawned in his ministry. Jesus announces in word and act that the promised kingdom is being realized in his person. Yet the eschatological promises are not exhausted in what he is doing; he anticipates a fulfillment of his ministry that is yet to come. After his passion and resurrection, the early community of faith proclaims his life as manifesting God's decisive act of grace, and its members eagerly confront men with a call to decide for him who is the Way. They look back upon what God has done in Jesus

Christ. *Yet they always anticipate a further act of God in the future.*

Why? If Jesus Christ was the decisive event, why should they look for anything more? The point is, Jesus and the earliest Christians understood well enough that the kingdom of God is never complete in this history of ours. Though it comes in so decisive a manner in Jesus of Nazareth that men are called upon to decide their lives in light of his life, no one can ever say with finality " 'Lo, here it is!' or 'There!' for behold, the kingdom of God is in the midst of you" (Luke 17:20). The kingdom is in the midst of men as a divine process that is continually realized wherever men speak and act with fidelity and wholeness. In Jesus of Nazareth we behold the consummate personalization of divine kingship, but Jesus does not exhaust the possibilities of God's reign. That is why he is raised in the kerygma to the cosmic level of Lord and Christ, for the early Christians intimate the cosmic dimensions of his person. The healing power of God's kingdom which he realized in his historical life is the power he as Lord and Christ is now bestowing upon the church. This power to make men whole is a process now being realized, and yet to be realized. The kingdom is not "here" or "there" to be seen once and for all in completed form: it is a dynamis in process, full of future possibility.

Accordingly, Luke can write to Theophilus that in his first book, the Gospel, he has "dealt with all that Jesus *began* to do and teach, until the day when he was taken up" (Acts 1:1 f.). The apostle Paul writes in the same vein: "And I am sure that he who *began* a good work in you will bring it to completion at the day of Jesus Christ" (Phil. 1:6). The punctiliar event of Jesus Christ is both historical and historic. The works Jesus did, the words he spoke, the person he was, is so crucial to the understanding of human existence that his significance goes far beyond the limits of his space and time, and enters our own where the possibilities are presented to us again and again in his person. The historical Jesus thus becomes the historic Christ, whose ministry of healing is always a new beginning as well as a continuation, with a future full of promise.

Are we then to think of a fulfillment of history, a Second Coming of Christ when this world is to be dissolved into a new heaven and a new earth (Rev. 21:1)? Millenarians in the church have looked for the end of the world since early times, and even today they are a strong voice in the community of Christians. We must not discount them in spite of their excesses. They tend to slight the social application of the gospel in preference to strong words about a heaven and hell to come. And they appear to know in great detail what will happen at the consummation, as though there were little mystery about it.

Yet they serve to remind us of the future dimension of the kingdom. Those who lose themselves in the importance of the present, who forget the past and let the future take care of itself, find themselves cut off and adrift, without landmarks, without direction. The person who has no point of reference but the present, even if he is a religious man, soon finds himself lost, despondent, cynical, and unbelieving. The answer to the present cannot be found in the present alone, but must derive from the past and the future.

The man of eschatological faith always finds his bearings between these two points. Like the great prophets of the Old Testament, he looks back to the nodular acts of God in the past and, believing that God has acted there (and that he works in the present), affirms that God will act in the future in a way analogous to those great events of the past. That is the eschatological understanding of time which is so characteristic of Jesus and his interpreters.

The Christian who stands in this eschatological tradition finds his bearings in the present by looking back to the great creative passage that God has made into the world of men in Jesus Christ. Jesus becomes the decisive event for him, be-

190

cause he is confronted with the decision to accept Jesus' wholeness and to become free. The fidelity of Jesus becomes a genuine possibility for him in the present. He experiences Jesus as the Christ who is always in process of redeeming the time and making him and other men whole.

And it is just for this reason, as he looks back to God's great act of grace in Jesus Christ and relives that personal act in his own life, that he anticipates the future action of God in the divine process of reconciliation. Jesus declared that the time of wholeness had come in his ministry, yet he looked for an even fuller manifestation of the Father's grace in the future. The early Christians looked back to what God had done in the life, death, and resurrection of Jesus, yet they anticipated the future completion of the good work God had begun in his Suffering Servant. And that is true of every eschatological man who claims and proclaims Christian faith. He discovers his freedom, hence himself, between the two polarities of God's saving work. The kingdom of God is an eschatology in process of realization within the three dimensions of time.

But some answer must be given the questions of how and when the consummation will take place. Great seas of ink have failed to answer these inquiries. We must remind ourselves that not a bit of our knowing, not even the tiniest jot is without its mystery. We should hardly expect the details of a cosmic event to be revealed in advance. Those who would chart the future with precision forget the mystery that surrounds our knowledge of God, the world, other persons—even ourselves. And they forget that the freedom of God and the freedom of men leaves the future open in detail. The not yet is possibility, not detailed certainty.

Only one thing is certain about the future, says the eschatological man: The God of fidelity and steadfast love will be present in every future as it passes into the present, offering himself as the ground of every creative word, act, and intention. Fidelity and wholeness will always be future possibilities because God is the faithful God of the past, the present, and the future. The man of faith can only imagine what this future of promise will be like. He has to express his hope in metaphors that are analogous to his knowledge of God's activity in the past and the present. He may imagine it as Christ's descending from heaven "with a cry of command, with the archangel's call, and with the sound of the trumpet of God" (1 Thess. 4:16); or as "the holy city, new Jerusalem, coming down out of heaven from God, prepared as a bride adorned for her husband" (Rev. 21:2). These are metaphorical exclamations of faith, and they bear likeness to Jesus' imaginative comparison of the kingdom of God to a great banquet which is now going on, but to which all the guests have not yet been invited (Luke 14:15-24); or to the coming of the Son of man, who will come as quickly as the lightning, and like the sudden flood in the days of Noah (Matt. 24:27, 37-39).

Yet the time is never stated: "But of that day and hour no one knows, not even the angels of heaven, nor the Son, but the Father only" (Matt. 24:36); "Therefore you also must be ready; for the Son of man is coming at an hour you do not expect" (Matt. 24:44).

Why is the hour unknown? Because Jesus and the early Christians do not display apocalyptic curiosity about the time, place, and manner of God's new visitation, but make affirmation only that the future belongs to God. And because it belongs to him, every present moment should be lived with purest integrity and fidelity as though it were the last hour before his coming: "Therefore you also must be ready." Repeatedly, it is readiness, wholeness, purity in the present that concerns Jesus and his followers. Because the future belongs to God, it holds no fear for men of faith. They are freed to live creatively in the present, because the future is full of promise. But the man who faces the abyss of the future without faith, in utter alienation, has lost the present. He is enervated by fear; he is lost to the present and to himself. No person can be whole who cannot cope with the future: Only the man who faces the future with confidence free of fear can live in the present with creative fidelity.[2]

What more do we need to know than this, that God will be in all our futures, whether they come in sudden cataclysm, like the lightning and the flood, or slowly and quietly, like the seed growing mysteriously? That is all we need to know, nothing more.

But we must die: What of that, you will ask? Yes, we must die. That is one future certainty we all must face. One day this "I" will no longer be. And when I die, the world dies with me; the abyss of nothingness—total alienation from every relation—will engulf me. Yet men refuse to believe in the total cessation of the self. If they do not speak of the immortality of the soul or of a resurrection from the dead, they believe that the world will go on after them, or they talk of an immortality through their progeny and in the continuation of their words and deeds. Or they describe immortality, as Charles Hartshorne does in one of the curious sections of his philosophy, as "everlasting fame before God."[3] When I die, he writes, the book of my self-awareness is closed forever; death is the ineluctable limit set on my life. But death does not destroy all that I have said and done between the covers of the book that is my life; no, God "resurrects" the life I have lived, the only life I ever will live, and incorporates it in his eternal and ever-increasing memory of all things terrestrial. God lives on as absolute self-consciousness, but I do not, except in his memory.[4]

Small solace, we may remark, to think that God will enjoy or sorrow in us forever—but in us as memories not as living persons. Is that the promise of the kingdom of God, is that the meaning of Jesus' resurrection and the resurrection hope that is inextricably a part of Christian faith? Certainly it is one aspect of it: All that we become in this life will be carried on in the eternal memory of God. But that does not even touch upon the other dimension of resurrection faith. Christian faith affirms the hope that though we die, death has lost its sting. It has lost its sting because God has raised Jesus from the dead, and will resurrect us by an act of grace and power analogous to the resurrection of Christ. The earliest witnesses to Jesus Christ affirm their fellowship with him after his resurrection from the dead (1 Cor. 15:3-8). They declare that by the dynamis of God his person, his "I" was raised again to consciousness into a new dimension of personal existence and fellowship. Paul presents this great hope in 1 Corinthians 15, asserting that if the self is not raised by God, then Christ was not raised; then Christian preaching and faith is vain, and "we are even found to be misrepresenting God" (1 Cor. 15: 12-19). "But in fact," Paul declares, "Christ *has* been raised from the dead." He has become the firstfruits of those who die, the second Adam who brings life where there is death (1 Cor. 15:20-23).

For Paul there is no immortality of the soul, no belief that some interior substance leaves the material body behind to make its claim before God. Paul's psychology is soundly incarnate. The self is inseparable from the unity of body and mind. Therefore, though the person is raised to a higher dimension of personal existence, it is his *self* which is raised from death to that new consciousness. Paul cannot express this hope without resorting to metaphor and mystery. It is like the seed that dies in the ground and is given a new body by God (1 Cor. 15:35-38); it is a *sōma pneumatikon,* a spiritual body, which will bear the image of "the man of heaven" as our present bodies have borne the image of Adam, the "man of dust" (1 Cor. 15:42-50).

These are not literal descriptions. They are metaphorical affirmations of faith in God's power to raise the self to new existence. And not only the self, but selves—all who seek him and love him, who desire to eat at the banquet of the kingdom. Resurrection is the *corporate* newness of life which can only be described as fellowship with God and his people. To be is to be together—that is the theme of the kingdom and the church; and to be raised is to be resurrected to a new fellowship. One of the gifts of grace, perhaps the greatest, is the promise that we will "all attain to the unity of the faith and of the knowledge of the Son of God, to mature manhood, to the measure of the stature of the fullness of Christ" (Eph. 4:13). True, this attaining begins in the present, but it anticipates a fulfillment: until we all attain, the apostle says.

Is the resurrection then to be a new discovery of the dimensions of fellowship, a continued activity of the "body" of Christ in future chapters of personal and corporate existence? That is certainly more in keeping with eschatological hope than the concept of a timeless, eternal now. Perhaps we are to think metaphorically of a beatific vision which is a continued process of joyful discovery of God and his creation, together with God's own enjoyment of every self in an unfolding fellowship of the Head and every member of his cosmic body.[5]

"That God may be everything to every one" (1 Cor. 15: 28)—that is the resurrection hope. "For he has made known to us in all wisdom and insight the mystery of his will, according to his purpose which he set forth in Christ as a plan for the fullness of time, to unite all things in him *(anakephalaiōsasthai ta panta en tō Christō),* things in heaven and things on earth" (Eph. 1:9 f.).

The gathering together of all things (the *anakephalaiōsis*) and the return of all things to God (the *apokatastasis,* Acts 3:21) that he may be all in all—is this not the Christian longing for the fellowship banquet of the kingdom, when all individual selves will exist in solidarity and society, like the union of cells in the human organism (1 Cor. 12:27)?[6] Yes, that is the hope of the kingdom, a mutual and continual participation of God and those who love him. And those who do not, who are alienated from him and his body? Are they not also numbered among the "all men" Paul speaks of to whom Christ has brought acquittal from the guilt of the past, and life for the future to come (Rom. 5:18)?

There are so many questions, and the mystery is so unfathomable. Yet the man of faith affirms the tremendous declaration of the earliest Christians: God will work in the future as he has in the resurrection of Christ; the future belongs to him. The eschatological man lives always in anticipation of the goal *(telos)* of the universe, when Christ "delivers the kingdom to God the Father after destroying every rule and every authority and power. . . . When all things are subjected to him, then the Son himself will also be subjected to him who put all things under him, that God may be everything to every one" (1 Cor. 15:24, 28).

Does not this metaphorical language express the eternal desire of God to realize the fellowship of all beings? As God has brought his wholeness among men through the universal gospel of Jesus Christ and has begun the good work of reconciling them all, Jew and Greek, slave and free, male and female, so has he promised to continue this good work of healing until the whole creation ceases from its groaning in travail (Rom. 8:18-23). In this way we may understand the hope of the early church, that what God has begun he will complete at the *eschaton,* the Omega Point, to use Teilhard de Chardin's expression, when this prodigious biological operation and the great family of the kingdom will be fulfilled, when the personal God of love consummates the process of redeeming incarnation.[7]

In this hope, men of faith are set free to redeem the present. As imitators of Christ, as men of wholeness and fidelity in word and deed they are free to redeem the world, to realize in the present the desire of God that every man participate in the fellowship of the kingdom, and become whole again.

196

That is the prayer of Jesus, who taught his disciples to pray,

Thy kingdom come
Thy will be done
On earth
As it is in heaven.

READINGS ON CHAPTER EIGHT

Cullmann, Oscar. *Immortality of the Soul or Resurrection of the Dead? The Witness of the New Testament.* London: Epworth Press, 1958.

Hartshorne, Charles. *The Logic of Perfection and Other Essays in Neoclassical Metaphysics.* La Salle, Ill.: Open Court Publishing Co., 1962.

Marcel, Gabriel. *Creative Fidelity.* Translated by Robert Rosthal. New York: Noonday Press, 1964.

May, Rollo (ed.). Existential Psychology. New York: Random House, 1961.

Polanyi, Michael. *Personal Knowledge: Towards a Post-Critical Philosophy.* Harper Torchbooks; New York: Harper & Row, 1964.

Teilhard de Chardin, Pierre. *The Phenomenon of Man.* Harper Torchbooks; New York: Harper & Row, 1961.

Unamuno, Miguel de. *The Tragic Sense of Life.* Translated by J. E. C. Flitch. New York: Dover, 1954.

Notes

CHAPTER ONE

1. Michael Polanyi has written his brilliant epistemological study, *Personal Knowledge: Towards a Post-Critical Philosophy* (Harper Torchbooks; New York: Harper & Row, 1964), around this central idea. All knowledge is personally accredited, or fiduciary, knowledge. See also his recent work, *The Tacit Dimension* (New York: Doubleday, 1966), which is suggested as an introduction to his thought.

2. Gabriel Marcel, *Creative Fidelity*, trans. Robert Rosthal (New York: Noonday Press, 1964), p. 183.

3. On the theme of copresence, see Marcel, *ibid.,* pp. 18, 32 f., 149. Coming to know someone of the past is not so different as one might think from knowing a present embodied person. In either case what are presented to us are clues or signs through which we intuit the unity of the person. So long as we focus upon the clues, we miss the wholeness of the one we wish to know. Then suddenly the clues become peripheral, and with an intuitive grasp we attend *through* and *from* the clues to a new dimension of the person we had not seen before. Signs and clues, when they function properly, move us on to some larger whole. They are transparent, diaphanous; they have a "tending toward" that beckons us on to intuit a greater unity. Michael Polanyi writes very effectively of attending from and attending to (the proximal and the distal, respectively), and the mysterious manner in which we always know more than we can tell—how we recognize a familiar face or idea, for instance. (See his recent study, *The Tacit Dimension* [New York: Doubleday, 1966] pp. 4-11). Paul Ricoeur, the French phenomenologist, is working along the same lines, particularly through the concept of feeling, which is the unifying moment of the whole. Feeling reveals intentionality and moves us from the less to the greater (*Fallible Man: Philosophy of the Will,* trans. Charles Kelbley [Chicago: Henry Regnery Company, 1965] pp. 129-137). This is essentially our position concerning the words and acts of Jesus, which are clues to his intentional self. There is, of course, one important difference between know-

ing a person of the past and someone embodied in the present, and it has to do with symmetry. We can intuit a person of the past through the clues that written signs afford us, but he cannot know us. He no longer has a capacity to respond to us; hence historical knowing is always asymmetrical. It moves from past to present but never from present to past. Contemporary embodied persons can respond to us; thus the relationship is reciprocal and symmetrical, giving us our sense of space as the former gives us our sense of time. (See Charles Hartshorne, "The Structure of Givenness," *The Philosophical Forum,* Vol. XVIII, 1960-61, pp. 22-39. For a brief and lucid presentation of this idea, see Eugene H. Peters, *The Creative Advance* [St. Louis: The Bethany Press, 1966] pp. 82-84.)

4. The problem of knowing how to decide which words and acts are authentically Jesus' own and not the christological interpretation of the early church is dealt with in a helpful manner by Van A. Harvey in *The Historian and the Believer* (New York: The Macmillan Company, 1966), pp. 265 ff. He suggests four levels of meaning of "Jesus of Nazareth" and their relationships to each other: (1) The actual Jesus as he lived his life in all its concreteness. The historian cannot hope to recover the actual Jesus because of the limits of human thought. (2) But some clues to his person are recoverable through historical study, and inferences may be made about this "historical Jesus." (3) To find the historical Jesus we must go to the documents which witness to him, and there we find a selection of clues, a "perspectival" or bas-relief approach, which is the "memory-impression" of Jesus by the earliest Christian community. This may or may not accord with (2), and Harvey is less than clear as to how the perspectival Jesus of (3) and the historical Jesus of (2) are related. (4) The biblical Christ is the fourth level and is quite easily identifiable. The early church is writing of Jesus in the cast of cosmic significance. The memory impression (3) has been altered by theological considerations, so that the Palestinian Jesus is, so to speak, unlocalized. Now he is the preexistent Logos, the virgin born, the omniscient miracle worker, the resurrected Christ, the fulfillment of Old Testament prophecies—in other words, the Johannine, cosmic Christ.

For simplicity, Harvey's levels may be reduced to two which concern us directly. The actual Jesus as he knew himself is not available to us any more than is the concreteness of any contemporary person, who always has a privileged access to himself that no one else can share exhaustively. Hence, the historian need not worry over the fact that he cannot exhaust the actual selfhood of persons past or present. All he needs are enough clues to enable him to intuit important dimensions of that actual self. These clues are confined here to level (3). Level (4) will be laid aside for the while because of the obvious christological heightening of the image of Jesus, although at points the shadings between (3) and (4) are not always clearly defined. That leaves levels (2) and (3). In order to arrive at the "historical" Jesus (2), the Jesus imaginatively intuited by historical inquiry, we shall have to rely upon the "perspectival" memory impression of Jesus given us by the early church. Harvey feels, justifiably, that in outline this image of Jesus' work and words is reliable (p. 269), though selective (as any image of another is bound to be).

But then, unfortunately, he makes the kind of logical howler that has marked the Bultmannian school for many years. After emphasizing how Jesus has the power to awaken the disciples, as a paradigm of God's action presents them with a new picture of life, teaches with authority and a peculiar ability, embodies God's sovereignty in his concern and deeds and words (pp. 270-272), he then makes the amazing remark that all this says nothing of Jesus' personal predilections or intentionality (p. 272). The only valid question is whether this man discloses God's intention for man— is his witness true or not (pp. 272 f.). This can be posed and answered without any reference whatsoever to Jesus' person (p. 274). This confusion comes of having a quite unsatisfactory concept of persons. If we follow Harvey's line of reasoning, we are permitted to speak at length of Jesus' concerns, his teaching and preaching and his conduct, but this gives us not the person Jesus but a witness, a word—a third-person abstraction. But what is a true witness? Can one say that it matters not at all what Jesus thought, but how well he witnessed to the truth? How does a person actually witness to the truth? Not, it is suggested here, by presenting an abstract set of historical beliefs, but by a personal life of trust and commitment to which words and actions are invaluable clues (cf. p. 280). Our study of Jesus' ministry maintains that the person Jesus is indispensable to Christian faith precisely because we do intuit him as an intentional person, as a person of wholeness, trust, and commitment, through his work and words. Not only is it schizophrenic to separate Jesus' witness to truth from his intentional self, but if this were carried out it would render him unnecessary, and Christianity would then become an abstract and timeless formula quite distant from the incarnational, personal emphasis given it by the early Christians. A great deal of Harvey's difficulty lies in the general historical skepticism of the day, with its hidden Kantian assumptions. Historians sometimes seem deeply disturbed because they cannot get hold of the whole historical person, as though that were possible even with contemporary selves with whom we have the added advantage of reciprocal relationships. Harvey remarks how badly off we are in New Testament studies with the scant material available for a knowledge of Jesus. American historians, he notes, are perplexed by Abraham Lincoln the person even though so much is available from his own hand (p. 193). In an appended footnote (p. 203, fn. 56) he remarks that one historian bemoans the difficulty of recovering the mind and personality of Lenin, though again so much of his own writing and the impressions of witnesses are available for critical study.

Accordingly, Harvey seems to be claiming that we cannot know the real Lincoln or the real Lenin, in spite of their personal writings and eyewitness accounts of the men. The case is all the stronger against knowing Jesus the person. The data is too sketchy and conflicting, he says. Thus, we can hardly claim to know the "real" Jesus. But think a moment: If those who "knew" Lincoln and Lenin are not able to communicate their images to us, perhaps they did not know these men at all. Does anyone, then, know anyone? What does it mean to know someone? And if both Lincoln and Lenin are unable to reveal themselves in their writings, are we not forever lost from their intentional selves—lost from them as persons, in other words? Then life is a series of appearances which overlie the real "things in themselves"—the old Kantian dilemma.

Is it not true, in actual fact, that coming to know other persons is a process of meeting one another? And that we never have others wholly in our possession at any time as they are in their total actuality? I may say of someone, "I know him but passingly," or "I know him well," or "I know him very well," but that does not mean I know him not at all in the first case, or exhaustively in the third case. The totality of another person is beyond my grasp: It is systematically elusive because it belongs exclusively to the privileged access a person has to himself. But there are important dimensions of our many-dimensioned selfhood that can be disclosed to others. These dimensions are revealed by the signs we speak and act out. When the signs are consistent, that is, when the speech signs do not contradict the action signs, they function mysteriously as aids to intuiting a new dimension of the person; the signs are then transparent and bear us on to intuit something far in excess of what the signs themselves can say. In the cases of Lincoln and Lenin, so many complementary facets are presented that the historian is perplexed by the utter complexity of these creative minds. It is not always an asset to have an abundance of signs—one is tempted to attend to them rather than through them.

Concerning Jesus of Nazareth, it seems that we have sufficient speech signs and action signs to allow us to intuit one especially important dimension of his person: that he was eminently one who sought a life of wholeness of intention, word, and act, and proclaimed that the kingdom of God is the sphere of wholeness, of redeeming compassion and justice, and of the solidarity of men, covenanted with God and one another. Jesus, then, is the parable and the key to reality (cf. Harvey, p. 283). Experienced by the disciples as the man of wholeness and healing, he came to be seen as the embodiment of wholeness and healing for every man, and so was raised to the new dimension of cosmic Lord and properly called Jesus the Christ.

5. Rudolf Bultmann, "The Primitive Christian Kerygma and the Historical Jesus," *The Historical Jesus and the Kerygmatic Christ: Essays on the New Quest of the Historical Jesus,* ed. Carl E. Braaten and Roy A. Harrisville (New York: Abingdon Press, 1964), p. 20.

6. *Ibid.,* p. 30.

7. *Ibid.,* pp. 22 f. Essentially the same things are said in Bultmann's earlier study *Jesus and the Word,* trans. L. P. Smith and E. H. Lantero (London: Fontana Books, 1958).

8. *Ibid.,* pp. 28 f.

9. *Ibid.,* pp. 27 f.

10. *Ibid.,* p. 42. Cf. Bultmann's *Theology of the New Testament* (London: SCM Press, 1952), I, 43. Bultmann has never quite recovered from Schweitzer's attack on the psychologizing distortions of Jesus by nineteenth-century interpreters. But in avoiding every hint to Jesus' psyche, he has perpetuated the fallacy that work and language can be separated from *persons.* In *Jesus and the Word* he emphatically argues that it is Jesus' *word,* and it alone, which comprehends his purpose (p. 15).

11. Maurice Merleau-Ponty, *Signs,* trans. Richard McCleary (Evanston, Ill.: Northwestern University Press, 1964), pp. 42 f.

12. Martin Heidegger, *Being and Time,* trans. J. Macquarrie and E. Robinson (New York: Harper & Row, 1962), p. 262.

13. Karl Jaspers, *The Origin and Goal of History* (New Haven: Yale University Press, 1963), Part I, chap. i.

14. Gerhard von Rad, *Old Testament Theology,* I, II, trans. D. M. G. Stalker (New York: Harper & Row, 1962, 1965). The punctiliar interpretation of history is also presented, with a fine sensitivity, by Abraham Heschel, *The Prophets* (New York: Harper & Row, 1962).

15. C. K. Barrett, *From First Adam to Last: A Study in Pauline Theology* (New York: Charles Schribner's Sons, 1962), p. 5.

CHAPTER TWO

1. See Joachim Jeremias, *The Parables of Jesus,* trans. S. H. Hooke (London: SCM Press, 1963), pp. 18-20, for a discussion of Jülicher's role in the interpretation of the parables.

2. Important discussions of the parable in the language of the New Testament are to be found in Amos Wilder, *The Language of The Gospel: Early Christian Rhetoric* (New York: Harper & Row, 1964), chapter V, and Robert Funk, *Language, Hermeneutic, and Word of God* (Harper & Row, 1966), chaps. 5-8.

3. Jeremias, *op. cit.,* pp. 13-18.

4. T. W. Manson, *The Teaching of Jesus* (Cambridge: Cambridge University Press, 1955), pp. 75-80.

5. Robert M. Grant, *A Historical Introduction to the New Testament* (New York: Harper & Row, 1963), pp. 348 f.

6. Helmut Thielicke, *The Waiting Father,* trans. John W. Doberstein (New York: Harper & Row, 1959). This is one of the finest collections of sermons on the parables.

7. Ernst Fuchs, "Jesus' Understanding of Time," *Studies of the Historical Jesus,* trans. Andrew Scobie ("Studies in Biblical Theology," No. 42 [London: SCM Press, 1964]), pp. 104-66. Unfortunately Fuchs suffers from the fallacy of the Bultmannian school which attempts to separate Jesus' ideas from Jesus the person. Fuchs is not really interested in Jesus as a person, but only in his understanding of time, an abstraction. Amos Wilder has ably criticized this deficiency in Fuchs' interpretation in "The Word as Address and the Word as Meaning," *New Frontiers in Theology,* Vol. II: *The New Hermeneutic,* ed. James M. Robinson and John B. Cobb, Jr. (New York: Harper & Row, 1964), p. 213.

8. Fuchs, *ibid.,* pp. 133 f.

CHAPTER THREE

1. Gabriel Marcel, "Observations on the Notions of the Act and the Person," *Creative Fidelity,* trans. Robert Rosthal (New York: Noonday Press, 1964), pp. 104-19.

2. Joachim Jeremias, *The Sermon on the Mount,* trans. Norman Perrin (Philadelphia: Fortress Press, 1963), pp. 19-23.

3. *Ibid.,* pp. 24-33.

4. *Ibid.,* pp. 30 f.

5. Based on the text by J. M. Allegro, *Palestine Exploration Quarterly* (1954), 69-75.

6. From *The New English Bible, New Testament.* © The Delegates of the Oxford University Press and the Syndics of the Cambridge University Press 1961. Reprinted by permission.

7. The flexibility of the two Greek verbs is ably discussed by Robert F. Berkey, *"Eggizein, Phthanein* and Realized Eschatology," *Journal of Biblical Literature,* LXXXII (June, 1963), 177-87, where the same argument is set forth in detail.

8. See Frank W. Beare, *The Earliest Records of Jesus* (New York: Abingdon Press, 1962), p. 91.

9. Heinz Eduard Tödt, *The Son of Man in the Synoptic Tradition,* trans. Dorothea M. Barton (Philadelphia: Westminster Press, 1965), pp. 32-112; 113-40. A study entitled *Rediscovering the Teaching of Jesus* by Prof. Norman Perrin of the University of Chicago (New York: Harper & Row, 1967) is being published at approximately the same time as this volume. Dr. Perrin, who kindly shared his prepublication manuscript with me in time to allow this brief inclusion, has written one of the most important and thorough studies on the synoptic tradition in recent years. It is a work that will have to be taken into account by every serious student of the New Testament. I include a note on the book at this point because Perrin has gone beyond Tödt in his handling of the Son of man sayings.

Following a thoroughgoing form critical approach to the Gospels (technically, *Redaktionstheologie*), Perrin applies with relentless precision the principle that no synoptic saying is to be accepted as actually spoken by Jesus unless it can be shown beyond reasonable doubt that the saying is dissimilar to theological emphases in Judaism or the early church. Using this "criterion of dissimilarity" (pp. 39, 45), he attempts to illumine the peculiar theological tendencies of the evangelists to heighten sayings, freely create new sayings, and apply them to Jesus. According to this technique of defining *Tendenzen,* no saying of Jesus is to be accepted as authentic unless the critic is forced to accept it as such: ". . . *the nature of the synoptic tradition is such that the burden of proof will be upon the claim to authenticity"* (p. 39, his italics). On this principle, the redaction method is applied with an even more critical eye than Tödt has used in his analysis of the Son of man sayings. The result is that Perrin cannot accept a single one of them as Jesus' own, not even the eschatological sayings which Tödt acknowledges to be genuine (see Perrin's discussion, pp. 164-85).

The critical method I have employed in interpreting the Son of man sayings in the next chapter is much less radical than Perrin's. I have tried to use criteria that clarify the dominical warrant and intention of Jesus, working first from the parables and gaining an appreciation of Jesus' creative molding of tradition and his free and open use of language. Then, having established what is characteristic of Jesus' action-speech, word-speech, and hence intention, I have tried to show a correlation with other sayings, in this case, with the Son of man material. Perrin's careful study must be weighed on its own merits, however; because of the open character of historical criticism he may be right, or nearer right than I am regarding the Son of man sayings. Even if he is correct, the main argument presented here is not appreciably altered. Professor Perrin and I have discussed the question together and agree that the sayings which redaction criticism affirms to be Jesus' own are adequate for the inquiry I am undertaking in this book. Dr. Perrin's concern is to establish authentic sayings that are beyond any doubt. Although I am not unconcerned with this question, my main purpose is to show that by using language analysis and contemporary studies on the phenomenology of persons, the irreducible minimum of authentic sayings (and acts) of Jesus are sufficient clues to enable us to intuit aspects of him as an intentional person. I would say, however, that if my argument is correct, features that are characteristic of Jesus' speech and activity may inform our opinion of other sayings which stand in the balance and may be tipped either way, depending on the critical presuppositions brought to them. Perrin appreciates this point (see his remarks, pp. 43 f., 238-48), although he is concerned lest the difference between faith statements and presuppositions and objective historical inquiry be blurred. He may be going too far in his claims for objective historical inquiry, however.

There is no question that the early church was at work, assimilating the sayings of Jesus to its own faith, problems, and expectations. But we disagree as critics over the degree to which the church transformed and created sayings of Jesus. If, as Perrin says, the early church was free and loose with Jesus' sayings because he himself set the pattern in his own speech, thereby giving them dominical warrant, then it seems terribly important to remember this background of dominical warrant before excusing a saying as church created. Linguistic and redaction arguments can be made to dismiss all the Son of man sayings, but if the criterion of dissimilarity is applied, no precise precedent for the manner in which the title is used in the Synoptics can be found either in Judaism or in the apostolic writings. It seems more likely that Jesus creatively employed the expression himself, giving warrant for its later free use by the early church. Though the church does not always or even often give us the *ipsissima verba* of Jesus, it does allow us to hear his warrant, pattern and voice, the *ipsissima vox*. Otherwise, we are guilty of supposing that the centers of the early church were more imaginative and creative than Jesus himself—a historical possibility, of course, but more conducive to gnostic than to incarnational Christianity.

But I have another and equally serious reservation about the mechanical application of the criterion of dissimilarity. It assumes a radical discontinuity between Jesus' indebtedness to the Old Testament and Judaism, and the early church's indebtedness to the language and activity of Jesus. But suppose Jesus is deeply indebted to Old Testament ways of thinking, speaking, and acting (as I believe he is), and the early church to the word-speech and action-speech of Jesus. Does it not beg the question to assume too radically that we can arrive at authentic sayings of Jesus only by discounting the lines of continuity? Helpful as the standard of dissimilarity may be in arriving at authentic sayings for which there is a high degree of probability, it is clear that it is hardly an objective scientific principle, but one which reflects the spirit of an age. It says as much about the critic and the day as it does about Jesus and the early church. In Perrin's inventive and ingenious study there can be seen a continuation of the Kantian model of doubt, for ours is an age that can bring itself to believe only an absolute minimum: "When in doubt, discard" (p. 11). Not that we ought to go to the other extreme, but perhaps we should appreciate how much we may lose of the whole when we focus upon a single-line standard of criticism.

In any event, the biblical scholar must hold literary criticism in perspective and with a certain sense of humor, lest he claim too much for his method of interpretation. We would do well to refer occasionally to Michael Polanyi's chapters on "The Logic of Affirmation," "The Critique of Doubt," and "Commitment" in *Personal Knowledge* (Harper Torchbooks; New York: Harper & Row, 1964), pp. 249-324, which may serve to remind us of the dangers of supposing that we are being quite objective when we are actually deeply involved as affirming persons in our interpretations. The actual facts are facts which are accredited by someone, within a situation of commitment.

10. I am indebted to Jeremias' sensitive remarks on these "children sayings" in *The Parables of Jesus,* trans. S. H. Hooke (London: SCM Press, 1963), pp. 190 f.

11. Augustine, *De libero arbitrio,* Book I, par. 4: "The steps are laid down by the prophet who says, 'Unless ye believe, ye shall not understand.' " Polanyi gives credit to Augustine for inaugurating for the first time a truly post-critical philosophy. Polanyi calls this "the logic of affirmation," and describes it as a "fiduciary program," *Personal Knowledge: Towards a Post-Critical Philosophy* (Harper Torchbooks; New York: Harper & Row, 1964), pp. 264-66.

CHAPTER FOUR

1. Heinz Eduard Tödt, *The Son of Man in the Synoptic Tradition,* trans. Dorothea M. Barton (Philadelphia: Westminster Press, 1965), pp. 224 f.

2. Albert Camus, *The Rebel: An Essay on Man in Revolt,* trans. Anthony Bower (New York: Vintage Books, 1962), p. 303.

3. *Ibid.,* p. 305.

4. *Ibid.,* p. 304.

5. *Ibid.,* pp. 304-6.

6. Ernst Käsemann, *Essays on New Testament Themes,* trans. W. J. Montague ("Studies in Biblical Theology," No. 41 [London: SCM Press, 1964; distributed in the U. S. by Alec R. Allenson, Inc.]), pp. 37-42.

7. *Ibid.,* p. 43. Used by permission.

8. For example, see James M. Robinson, "The Recent Debate on the 'New Quest,' " *The Journal of Bible and Religion,* XXX (July, 1962), 202, where the author is careful to distinguish between the understanding of existence which emerges from Jesus' activity, and Jesus' self-understanding of that activity.

9. Ludwig Wittgenstein, *Philosophical Investigations,* trans. G. E. M. Anscombe (New York: Macmillan, 1964), pp. 183, 217, 219, 225, 228, e.g.

10. Frank W. Beare, *The Earliest Records of Jesus* (New York: Abingdon Press, 1962), p. 77.

11. *Ibid.,* p. 186.

12. Günther Bornkamm, *Jesus of Nazareth,* trans. Irene and Fraser McLuskey, with James M. Robinson (New York: Harper & Row, 1960), p. 81.

13. See also Reginald H. Fuller, *The Mission and Achievement of Jesus* ("Studies in Biblical Theology," No. 12 [London: SCM Press, 1954]), p. 99.

14. See *ibid.,* pp. 55 f.

CHAPTER FIVE

1. Gabriel Marcel, *Creative Fidelity,* trans. Robert Rosthal (New York: Noonday Press, 1964), p. 107.

2. *Ibid.,* pp. 109-13.

3. *Ibid.,* p. 40.

4. Alfred North Whitehead, *Adventures of Ideas* (New York: Macmillan, 1948), chap. xiii. Charles Hartshorne, *The Logic of Perfection and Other Essays in Neoclassical Metaphysics* (La Salle, Ill.: Open Court Publishing Co., 1962), chap. iii.

5. Edgar Hennecke, *New Testament Apocrypha,* ed. Wilhelm Schneemelcher, trans. R. McL. Wilson (Philadelphia: Westminster Press, 1963), I, 363-417.

6. See Ernst Käsemann, *Essays on New Testament Themes,* trans. W. J. Montague ("Studies in Biblical Theology," No. 41 [London: SCM Press, 1964]), pp. 39 f.

7. From *Personal Knowledge,* by Michael Polanyi, copyright © Harper & Row, Publishers, Inc. 1964 Torchbook edition, p. 318. Used by permission of Harper & Row and Routledge & Kegan Paul Ltd.

8. Cf. Joachim Jeremias, *Jesus' Promise to the Nations,* trans. S. H. Hooke ("Studies in Biblical Theology," No. 24 [London: SCM Press, 1958]), pp. 57 ff.

9. Dom Gregory Dix, *Jew and Greek* (New York: Harper & Row, n.d.), p. 108.

10. F. W. Beare, *The Earliest Records of Jesus* (New York: Abingdon Press, 1962), p. 225.

11. Rudolf Bultmann, "The Primitive Christian Kerygma and the Historical Jesus," *The Historical Jesus and the Kerygmatic Christ: Essays on the New Quest of the Historical Jesus,* ed. Carl E. Braaten and Roy A. Harrisville (New York: Abingdon Press, 1964), pp. 23 f.

12. Schubert M. Ogden, "Bultmann and the 'New Quest,' " *The Journal of Bible and Religion* (now *the Journal of the American Academy of Religion;* pub. at Philadelphia), XXX (July,

1962), 210. Used by permission. Also see James M. Robinson, "The Recent Debate on the 'New Quest,' " *ibid.,* p. 202.

13. See Michael Polanyi's chapters, "The Logic of Affirmation," "The Critique of Doubt," and "Commitment," in *Personal Knowledge: Towards a Post-Critical Philosophy,* pp. 249-324.

14. From *Christ Without Myth,* by Schubert Ogden, copyright © Schubert M. Ogden 1961, p. 159. Used by permission of Harper & Row, Publishers, Inc.

15. Miguel de Unamuno, *The Tragic Sense of Life,* trans. J. E. C. Flitch (New York: Dover, 1954), pp. 136, 137.

16. C. H. Dodd, *According to the Scriptures* (London: Nisbet & Co., 1952; New York: Charles Scribner's Sons, 1953), p. 123, Used by permission of both publishers.

CHAPTER SIX

1. P. T. Forsyth, *The Person and Place of Christ* (London: Independent Press Ltd., 1955), pp. 122 f. Used by permission of the publisher and Mrs. Jessie Forsyth Andrews.

2. James Denney, *Jesus and the Gospel* (London: Hodder and Stoughton, 1908), pp. 25, 26.

3. See Charles Hartshorne, *The Logic of Perfection and Other Essays in Neoclassical Metaphysics* (La Salle, Ill.: Open Court Publishing Co., 1962), pp. 101 f., 141 f.

4. Anders Nygren, *Agape and Eros,* trans. Philip S. Watson (Philadelphia: Westminster Press, 1953).

5. C. H. Dodd, *Historical Tradition in the Fourth Gospel* (Cambridge: Cambridge University Press, 1963).

6. R. H. Lightfoot, *St. John's Gospel* (Oxford: Oxford University Press, 1956), p. 226.

7. E. G. Selwyn, *The First Epistle of St. Peter* (London: Macmillan, 1958), p. 124.

8. Cf. Phil. 1:6—"I am sure that he who began a good work in you will bring it to completion at the day of Jesus Christ."

CHAPTER SEVEN

1. See *The Church* by Karl Ludwig Schmidt (translated from Kittel's *Theologisches Wörterbuch zum Neuen Testament*) 1950. London: A. & C. Black Ltd.; New York: Harper & Row. Pp. 51 ff.

2. *Ibid.,* p. 16; cf. p. 21. Used by permission.

3. R. H. Fuller, "Church," *A Theological Word Book of the Bible,* ed. Alan Richardson (London: SCM Press, 1954; New York: The Macmillan Company, 1950), p. 48. Used by permission of both publishers.

4. See Charles Hartshorne, *The Logic of Perfection and Other Essays in Neoclassical Metaphysics* (La Salle, Ill.: Open Court Publishing Co., 1962), pp. 63 f., 66 ff., 93 f., 105 f.

5. From *Theological Essays,* by Frederick Denison Maurice, copyright © Harper & Brothers 1957, p. 60; cf. pp. 73, 94 ff., 207 ff., 331. Used by permission of Harper & Row, Publishers, Inc., and James Clarke & Co. Ltd.

CHAPTER EIGHT

1. See Gerhard von Rad, *Old Testament Theology* (New York: Harper & Row, 1965), II, 112-19.

2. See Abraham H. Maslow's remarks on the importance of future time in psychology, *Existential Psychology,* ed. Rollo May (New York: Random House, 1961), pp. 58 f.

3. Charles Hartshorne, *The Logic of Perfection and Other Essays in Neoclassical Metaphysics* (La Salle, Ill.: Open Court Publishing Co., 1962), p. 259.

4. See his chapter, "Time, Death, and Everlasting Life," *ibid.,* pp. 245-62.

5. See Miguel de Unamuno, "Religion, the Mythology of the Beyond and the Apocatastasis," *The Tragic Sense of Life,* trans. J. E. C. Flitch (New York: Dover, 1954), pp. 229, 243. Even the logician Hartshorne, though he personally prefers not to believe in any continuation of personal existence beyond death, allows that further chapters of life are possible. However, he does deny that the chapters could be infinite. This is a genuine impossibility, he reasons, because in an unlimited future time one would experience unlimited novelty, which would logically erase the distinction between being a creaturely self and being God (*The Logic of Perfection and Other Essays in Neoclassical Metaphysics,* pp. 253 f.). This is a subtle point, and one wonders how far this kind of logic should rule over the traditional Christian resurrection hope. The fact that Hartshorne chooses not to believe in the "logical" possibility of limited future chapters reveals his predilection

for his interpretation of resurrection. Here we see a striking example of how choices between logical possibilities are made on other than logical grounds; namely, through the emotional and fiduciary dimensions of knowledge, of which Polanyi has made us so aware. Biblical faith understands the resurrection to be the gift of continued *fellowship* with God and his people, not a hope that the self will become God. It also affirms that God has the freedom and the power to give this gift to men, and indeed will grant it, on the analogy of Christ's resurrection. The resurrection is first of all a *fiduciary* affirmation.

6. See Unamuno, *ibid.,* pp. 242-59.

7. Pierre Teilhard de Chardin, *The Phenomenon of Man* (Harper Torchbooks; New York: Harper & Row, 1961), pp. 257-63, 267-72, 287-88, 293-94. Perhaps it is better to think of the Omega Point as a divine ideal which God continually desires to achieve in the concrete process of redemption. The biblical idea of the banquet of the kingdom assumes a continuation of the process of time and experience, but on a higher, purified level. It may be the fellowship of God with his universe on this higher level that is suggested in the image of the Omega Point.

INDEXES

INDEXES

Index of Subjects and Authors

A

Abba, 86 f.
Act and gesture, in Marcel, 108
Acts of Jesus, 107-33
Agape: in Paul, 145-48; in John, 155 f.
Alienation, 121, 146
Amen, Jesus' use of, 95-7
Anakephalaiōsis, 195
Anxiety, freedom from, 68
Apocalyptic: Son of man, 90-2; theologians, 188
Apocryphal Infancy Gospels, 114
Apokatastasis, 195
Atonement, 130
Autobasileia, 28, 38
Axial Period, Jaspers on, 28

B

Banquet, of the kingdom, 124 f.
Baptism, of Jesus, 107-11
Bar-nasha, 72
Barrett, C. K., 30 f.
Beare, Frank W., 59, 88, 99, 133
Beatitudes, 68
Behavior, in 1 Peter, 160-62
Belief, in healing, 116
Berkey, Robert F., 205
Best, Ernest, 186
Body: metaphor in Paul, 146; of God, an organism, 195; of Christ, 175 f.

Bornkamm, Günther, 100
Braaten, Carl E., 31, 133
Bread, Jesus as, 151, 174
Bride, bridegroom, 39, 178-80
Building, metaphor of, 177 f.
Bultmann, Rudolf, 9 f., 23-5, 70, 75, 97 f., 127 f., 203

C

Caesarea Philippi, 81 f., 121
Cain, question of, 50
Camus, Albert, 92-4
Chiasmus, in Jesus' ministry, 126
Children, 86 f.
Christ: cosmic, 89; of faith, 137-72; life in (Paul), 142-49; Jesus as historic, 190
Christology, 24
Church: kerygma of, 139-41; in Paul, 147; of God, 180-84; an institution, 185 f.
Cobb, John B., Jr., 59, 106
Commitment, of the agent, 108
Community, in Hebrews, 168-70
Compassion, 58
Complementary aspection, 20, 62, 202
Conflict: in the parables, 43-58; of the kingdom, 77-9, 86
Consummation, of the kingdom, 187-97. *See also* Second Coming

217

Maslow, Abraham H., 211
Mass, Eastern and Western, on the
 Last Supper, 124
Maurice, Frederick Denison, 185
May, Rollo, 197
McArthur, Harvey K., 88
Merleau-Ponty, Maurice, 7, 9, 26
Messiah: Jesus' understanding of,
 56; his messianic claims, 66, 95-
 9; his messianic signs, 123
Metaphorical language, in the par-
 ables, 35
Miracles: Jesus', 114-20; nature of,
 118 f.
Mission of the Twelve, 119
Moses, Jesus the new, 65, 73
Munck, Johannes, 172
Mystery: Mark on the parables,
 35 f., of the kingdom in the par-
 ables, 51-4; of the resurrection,
 132, 196

N

Nathan and David, 44
Nationalism, kingdom not to be
 identified with, 122 f.
New English Bible, 70, 74
Niebuhr, Richard R., 133
Nygren, Anders, 147 f.

O

Ogden, Schubert, 127
Omega point, 196, 212
Origen, 28, 34
Ōthōth, 121-33

P

Panentheism, 175-77. *See also* Process; Hartshorne
Parables: of Jesus, 33-60; as elemental language, 25 f.; public
 situation of, 33; Nathan and
 David, 34 f.; of realization, 39-
 51; of growth and process, 51-4;
 of judgment and fulfillment, 55-
 9; physician, 41; patch and wine-
 skin, 41; two debtors, 42 f.; two
 sons, 43; Pharisee and the publican, 44 f.; lost sheep and lost
 coin, 45; prodigal son, 45 f.;
 tower builder and warring king,

47; "weighing" sayings, 47 f.;
 children in the marketplace, 48;
 the empty house, 48; laborers in
 the vineyard, 48 f.; good Samaritan, 50; great supper, 50 f.; seed
 growing mysteriously, 51 f.; the
 sower, 52 f.; mustard seed, 53;
 leaven, 53 f.; wheat and the
 weeds, 54; wicked tenants, 55 f.;
 talents, 56; sheep and the goats,
 56 f.; waiting servants, thief at
 night, ten maidens, 57; unsound
 eye, rich fool, 57; savorless salt,
 servant vested with authority, unmerciful servant, 58; two trees,
 two houses, 67; dramatized acts,
 121-33
Parousia, 141, 162-65
Participation, metaphors of, 185
Passover, and Last Supper, 124 f.
Paul, 53 f., 70, 131, 141-9
Perrin, Norman, 32, 205-08
Personal pronoun "I," 7-9. *See also*
 First- and second-person language
Persons: personal knowledge, epis-
 temology, 17-31, 87; words, acts,
 intention a unity, 126-28; knowl-
 edge of, 200
Perspectival memory-impression of
 Jesus (V. Harvey), 200-03
Persuasion, the way of the king-
 dom, 85
Peters, Eugene H., 10, 200
Pharisees and scribes: in the setting
 of the parables, 41-57; 63 f., 122
Phenomenology of persons, 126, 199
 f., 206
Philia, in John, 155 f.
Pilate, 129
Polanyi, Michael, 7-9, 37, 87 f.,
 117, 126, 199, 207
Political consciousness of Jesus, 112
Power, *en dynamei,* 74 f. *See also*
 Dynamis
Pragmatism, of the early commu-
 nity, 138 f.
Prayer: in healing, 116; Jesus, 154
Pride, hubris, 85 f.
Priest, Christ as, in Hebrews, 165-
 71

Index of Scripture References

OLD TESTAMENT